Also by Thomas Fensch . . .

The Kennedy-Khrushchev Letters

Orwell in America

Foreshadowing Trump:
      Trump characters, Ethics, Morality
      and Fascism in classic literature

... and others.

INSIDE

Nixon's Enemies List

THE WHITE HOUSE
WASHINGTON

Date: 9/17

TO: John Dean

FROM: GORDON STRACHAN

The attached should be of interest to you and the political enemies project.

Thomas Fensch

New Century Books

New Century Books
8821 Rockdale Rd.
N. Chesterfield, Va., 232136-2150
newcentbks@gmail.com

ISBN 978-1-7333293-0-9 (paperback)
ISBN 978-1-7333293-3-0 (ebook)

Note: The memo on the cover of this book and elsewhere in the text, from Gordon
Strachan to John Dean, has not been created or designed for this book. It was part of the
original Nixon enemies list archives, from the Nixon Administration. Although originally
in white, it is now printed in yellow on the cover to indicate that it would likely be a post-
it note or a sticky note today.

Additionally: Documents in this book, insofar as possible, are reprinted from original
sources. Type styles and sizes differ from the author's text and analysis.

Contents

1 Inside Nixon's Enemies List

For decades and decades now, perhaps since the American Civil War, when newspapers began transmitting articles from city to city by telegraph, print journalists have been guided by the *5 W's and the H.* techniques to write the beginning of a nonfiction article. The beginning, called the *lede,* pronounced *leed.* is the most crucial part of a news article. The *lede* capsulizes the article for the reader, often, but not always, in three brief paragraphs.

They are:

Who? Is the person famous, infamous, a notable person, known locally, regionally or nationally? Begin the article with that person by name.

What? What happened? Describe to the reader what happened to begin the article.

Where? Is the location important? Begin there.

When? When did the event begin? Is the time important? — when did D-Day began in France — when did other events began —

Why? Why did the story begin? The writer — a print, or a broadcast reporter — may have to explain the *why* to the reader.

How? How did this event happen? (Often the *why* or *how* of an complicated story are not apparent until weeks or months later; an airliner crash, for instance. The *how did this crash happen?* may not be apparent until the aircraft "black boxes'" can be found and examined for engine failure, weather conditions or other contributing factors to a crash.)

In *One Man Against the World: The Tragedy of Richard Nixon.* Tim Weiner writes:

> Richard Nixon led the United States through a time of unbearable turmoil. He made war in pursuit of peace.He committed crimes in the name of the law. He tore the country apart while trying to unite it. He sabotaged his presidency by violating the Constitution. He destroyed himself and damaged the nation through deliberate acts of folly.
>
> He vowed to bring the tragedy of Vietnam to an honorable end; he brought death and disgrace instead. He practiced

geopolitics without subtlety; he preferred subterfuge and brutality. He dropped bombs and napalm without remorse; he believed they delivered a political message beyond blood and fire. He charted the course of the war without a strategy; he delivered victory to his adversaries.

* * *

Yet he had an undeniable greatness, an unsurpassed gift for the art of politics, an unquestionable desire to change the world. He wielded power like a Shakespearean king.

In his eyes, he stood above the law, and that was his fatal flaw, for he fell like a king fated to die in the final act of a tragedy. His arrogation of power created the criminal conduct that his White House counsel warned him was a "cancer within, close to the presidency, that's growing. It's growing daily."

The White House counsel who warned Nixon about a cancer on the presidency was John Dean.

Richard Nixon's childhood and family life might easily be called California hardscrabble. He was born January 9, 1913 in Yorba Linda, California, the second of five boys (four of the five named for British kings: Harold; Richard; Francis Donald; Arthur and Edward. Richard was named after Richard the Lionhearted.) His younger brother Arthur died in 1928 after a short illness and his older brother, Harold, whom he admired, died in 1933 of tuberculosis.

In his last speech, before the assembled White House staff, just before he left by helicopter for the last time, he said:

I remember my old man. I think that they would have called him sort of a little man, common man. He didn't consider himself that way. You know what he was? He was a streetcar motorman first, and then he was a farmer, and then he had a lemon ranch... And then he was a grocer. But he was a great man, because he did his job, and every job counts up to the hilt, regardless of what happens.

* * *

Nobody will ever write a book, probably, about my mother. Well, I guess all of you will say this about your mother — my mother was a saint. And I think of her, two boys dying of tuberculosis, nursing four others in order that she could take care of my older brother for three years in Arizona, and seeing each of them die.... Yes, she will have no books written about her, but she was a saint.

One spectator, David Ransom, a Marine veteran, called Nixon's rambling, self-absorbed, last speech "pathetic."

And what of his father, the "common man"? He left his job as a streetcar motorman in Columbus, Ohio, after sustaining frostbite in an open streetcar. In California, despite his work, the family became impoverished and he was left "a restless, frustrated and angry man, a mean-spirited person who psychologically abused his five sons and sometimes beat them." Nixon called his mother a "saint" or "a Quaker saint." His father, originally a Methodist, became a Quaker when he married Nixon's mother.

His mother's Quaker background forbade alcohol, swearing and dancing.

Although Nixon apparently never did, we can describe this family as dysfunctional, based largely on the behavior of Nixon's father and his mother's Quaker religion.

Nixon attended high school in Fullerton, California, then Whittier, California. At that time, his brother Harold had been diagnosed with tuberculosis and his mother took him to Arizona for the drier climate; Richard's obligations at home increased but he was able to graduate on time; third in his class of 207 students.

He was offered a tuition grant to attend Harvard, but travel costs would have been overwhelming for the family and he was still needed at home; he consequently attended nearby Whittier College, a Quaker college, paid for by a bequest from his maternal grandfather. He graduated in 1934 and was offered a full scholarship to Duke University Law School, then attempting to attract top students with full scholarships, which were reduced during their second and third years. Nixon kept his scholarship for all three years and graduated in June, 1937.

After Duke, he attempted to join the FBI, but got no response to his letter of application; he later learned that he had been accepted by the FBI, but the position was lost as a result FBI budget cuts.

He was admitted to the California bar in 1937 and joined the law firm of Wingert and Bewley, working on litigation for California petroleum companies. He was reluctant to work on divorce cases because he didn't want hear frank sexual talk, especially from women. He became a full partner in the firm in 1939.

Previously, in January 1938, he was cast in the Whittier Community Players production of the play "The Dark Tower" and met a high school teacher, Thelma "Pat" Ryan. He said it was love at first sight for him, but apparently not for her. She said no several times before even dating him once. They dated for two years before she accepted his marriage proposal; they were married in a small ceremony June 21, 1940. They had two daughters Tricia, born in 1946 and Julie, in 1948. The Nixons stayed married throughout his career; Pat Nixon died June 22, 1983, at 81.

In January, 1942, the Nixons moved to Washington, D.C., where Nixon took a job at the Office of Price Administration. In his political campaigns, Nixon suggested, or implied, that this was his response to Pearl Harbor, but he had sought the position during the last half of 1941. Both Nixon and his wife believed he was limiting his opportunities by staying in Whittier. He was assigned to the tire rationing division, where he had to reply to incoming correspondence He did not enjoy that role and after four months, applied to join the Navy.

As a birthright Quaker, he could have sought an exemption from the draft; he also could have sought an exception because he was working in government service. But he sought a commission in the Navy; he was appointed a lieutenant junior grade in the U.S. Naval Reserve June 15,1942.

In October, 1942, he was assigned as aide to the commander of the Naval Air Station Ottumwa, in Iowa, until May, 1942,. Seeking more than a stateside assignment, he requested sea duty and on July 2, 1943, was assigned to Marine Aircraft Group 25 and the South

Pacific Combat Air Transport Command (SCAT) supporting the logistics of operations into South Pacific Theater. On October 1, 1943, Nixon was promoted to lieutenant; he commanded the SCAT forward detachments at Vella Lavella, Bougainville and finally at Green Island (Nissan Island).

His unit prepared manifests and flight plans for R4D/ C-47 operations and supervised the loading and unloading of the transport aircraft. For this service, he received a Navy Letter of Commendation (awarded a Navy Commendation Ribbon, which was later updated to the Navy and Marine Corps Commendation Medal) from his commanding officer for "meritorious and efficient performance of duty as Office in Charge of the South Pacific Combat Air Transport Command."

Upon his return to the U.S., Nixon was appointed the administrative officer of the Alameda Naval Air Station in California. In January, 1945, he was transferred to the Bureau of Aeronautics office in Philadelphia to help negotiate the termination of war contracts, and received his second letter of commendation, from the Secretary of the Navy, for "meritorious service, tireless effort, and devotion to duty." Later, he was transferred to other offices to work on contracts. He was finally transferred to Baltimore. On October 3, 1945, he was promoted to lieutenant commander. On March 10, 1946, he was relieved of active duty. He resigned his commission on New Years Day, 1946. On June 1, 1953, he was promoted to commander; he retired from the U.S. Naval Reserve on June 6, 1966.

Nixon won the first political race he entered, in 1946; 22 years later, after suffering major, catastrophic political defeats, he was elected President; the 37th President of the United States.

While still in the east, in late 1945, he received a call; would he return to California and enter the Congressional race against popular Democratic candidate, Jerry Vorhiss? He was nominated by a branch manager of the Whittier Bank of America, who knew Nixon. The Nixons talked the idea over and by the next day agreed to return to California. In early 1946, he began an intense year-long campaign. He suggested that Vorhiss had been ineffective as a congressman and had accepted funds from a group linked to communism, thereby implying that Vorhiss must have radical views. Nixon received 65,586 votes to 49,994 for Vorhiss. He learned from his first experience; it would not be the last time he would invoke the specter of communism regarding political opponents.

In February, 1947, he joined the House Un-American Activates Committee (commonly abbreviated HUAC). His maiden speech in Congress focused on enemies to the HUAC committee. He had his name on a (Karl) Mundt-Nixon bill, in 1948, which provided for registration of all known

Communist party members and required a source of all printed and broadcast material believed to be issued by communist front organizations. The bill passed the House of Representatives 319 to 88 votes, but failed to pass in the Senate; it was, however, still considered Nixon's first congressional victory.

Nixon first gained national attention in August, 1948, when his persistence as a member of the HUAC committee helped break the Alger Hiss spy case. While many doubted Whittaker Chambers's allegations that Hiss, a former State Department official, had been a Soviet spy, Nixon believed them to be true and pressed for the committee to continue its investigation. Under suit for defamation filed by Hiss, Chambers produced documents corroborating his allegations; these included paper and microfilm material that Chambers turned over to House investigators after having hidden them overnight in a field; they became known as the "Pumpkin Papers." Hiss was convicted of perjury in 1950 for denying under oath he had passed documents to Chambers.

Nixon had became known as one of the leading anti-Communist crusaders in Congress and would ride that issue onward.

In 1948, he successfully filed as a candidate for Congress for both political parties (called "cross-filing") and was comfortably reelected.

In 1949, he began considering as run for the U.S. Senate from California. Democratic incumbent Sheridan Downey, faced with a primary battle, announced his retirement in March 1950. Nixon then faced Helen Gahagan Douglas. It was a turning point, in at least one respect, for him.

Douglas shared much of the same voting record aa New York Congressman Vito Marcantino, who was believed by some to have Communist sympathies or Communist tendencies.

Nixon portrayed Douglas if not completely Communist "red," then least pink. A Communist fellow traveler, as was historically said or implied. Nixon issued a "pink sheet," with her voting record. He won by almost 20 points, but during that campaign was first called "Tricky Dick," which stayed with him throughout the rest of his life.

In the U.S. Senate, he continued his anti-communist zeal and criticized President Harry Truman's handling of the Korean War. He was in favor of statehood for Alaska and Hawaii, and favored civil rights legislation.

The Republican party nominated Dwight Eisenhower for President in 1952; he had no real preferences for a vice-presidential running mate.

Nixon, then 39, was thought a rising star in the G.O.P. His anti-Communist stance and his political base of California were seen as positives by the G.O.P.

In September, 1952, Nixon was faced with a crisis; the media reported that he had a secret slush fund, which reimbursed him for expenses. Such a fund was not illegal then, but exposed him to allegations of conflicts of interest. He went on national television September 23, 1952 and claimed that the fund was not secret, that donors had not received special favors and admitted that his wife did not have a mink coat, just a "respectable Republican cloth coat." (Pat Nixon later admitted feeling embarrassed when he revealed in the Checkers speech how little finances they had.) He did admit one gift — a donor in Texas had sent the family a cocker spaniel, which daughter Tricia, then six, had named "Checkers." And we'll keep it, he said. The "Checkers" speech was seen by 60 million Americans; the positive reception kept Nixon on the Republican presidential ticket with Eisenhower.

Eisenhower had a heart attack September 24, 1955 and his condition was first thought to be life-threatening. There was no clear line of succession at that time but Nixon performed admirably well for the six weeks it took for Eisenhower to recover.

Nixon remained Eisenhower's vice-president for eight years—Eisenhower's two full-terms, 1953-1961. The Eisenhower-Nixon team was re-elected by a comfortable margin in the November, 1956 national election, for Eisenhower's second term in the presidency.

In 1960 Nixon launched his first campaign for the presidency. He ran largely unopposed as a Republican and faced John Kennedy in the election. The campaign was close from the start. Kennedy claimed that the Eisenhower-Nixon administration had allowed the Soviet Union to overtake the U.S. in ballistic missiles.

This election was the first time presidential debates were televised nationally. Kennedy looked fresh, tanned and assured. Nixon looked haggard and apparently needed a shave. For those watching on television, Kennedy was the winner; for those listening on radio, Nixon appeared to have won.

John Kennedy won by the smallest margin in modern election history; he won the popular vote by 112,827 votes or .2 percent of the electorate.

At the end of January, 1961, when his term as part of the Eisenhower administration was over, Nixon returned to California, where he practiced law and wrote a book, *Six Crises*, which included the Hiss case. Eisenhower's heart attack and the scandal over the secret fund which culminated in the Checkers speech.

Two years after his loss to Kennedy, California Republican officials urged him to run against Pat Brown, in the up-coming race for Governor of California. Nixon was skeptical; if he lost, after losing to Kennedy, his political career would be over. But if he took the race; skeptics could charge that he did so simply as a stepping stone for another national political office.

Nixon lost the race to Pat Brown by more than five percent points and in a press conference the morning after the election Nixon blamed the press and famously said, "You won't have Nixon to kick around any more because, gentlemen, this is my last press conference."

Nixon was nothing if not tenacious; he had lost to John Kennedy and then to Pat Brown. Lyndon Johnson had become president following the assassination of Kennedy; but Johnson had become mired in the unending war in Vietnam. Johnson withdrew as a candidate for re-election in March, 1968, believing he could not win.

In June, Robert Kennedy was assassinated in California moments after securing the California Democratic primary; Hubert Humphrey became Nixon's Democratic rival; Humphrey's nomination convention in Chicago was married by massive demonstrations in the streets of Chicago and subsequently, throughout the nation, by anti-Vietnam war protestors.

Nixon appealed to what he called the "silent majority," of Americans who disliked the hippie, anti-Vietnam war culture throughout the country

The campaign was marred by accusations that Nixon was bargaining behind the scenes to end the war only after the election; thus betraying the Lyndon Johnson administration's efforts to end the war successfully

Nixon won by nearly 500,00 voters nationally and by 301 Electoral College votes to Humphrey's 191 and 46 for third party candidate George Wallace.

He was inaugurated as president January 20,1969 vowing to be a peace president and vowing to turn partisan political politics into unity

His clear mandate was solving the previously unsolvable problem of peace in Vietnam (which destroyed the presidency of Lyndon Johnson) ; he considered himself a world leader and grew to disdain domestic presidential politics, once famously equating domestic policies to "building outhouses in Peoria."

* * *

Returning to the journalistic *5 Ws and the H:* This is a *why* story. *Why* did Nixon and his people begin their "political enemies" project? Did they know it would surely be unethical? Or immoral? Controversial, surely? Did they know it might well have been illegal? What drove them to do this?

Simply stated: *why* did they do this?

In *One Man Against the World,* Tim Weiner writes:

> The President spent far more energy trying to destroy the cornerstones of the Great Society, particularly LBJ's grandest endeavor for the poor, the Office of Economic Opportunity. He ordered two young eager-beaver staffers, Dick Cheney and Don Rumsfeld (two future Secretaries of Defense), to attack the OEO, which included Head Start, for schooling young children; Legal Services, providing lawyers to the poor; VISTA, or Volunteers in Service to America, created as a domestic Peace Corps; and a wide varsity of health and education projects.

* * *

Nixon gave these men their first taste of executive power, and they liked it. They were proud foot soldiers in an army of young conservatives doing battle for the president.

"The Nixon administration came in disliking OEO intensely and I could never understand why Don took the job," said Frank Carlucci, another future Secretary of Defense, recruited by Rumsfeld. "They kept calling me and telling me to kill this or kill that."

Carlucci believed that the OEO had achieved one major success: "to provide upward mobility for the people who were poverty stricken and in the low-income brackets. An awful lot of the leadership came up through these programs," leaders who were not white men, "including people who became subsequently members of congress." A program that helped to produce black leaders was anathema to Nixon; the informal compendium of his political opponents that came to be known as the "the enemies list" contained every black member of Congress. The "OEO was the enemy," Carlucci concluded.

"There's not question there was a very strong emotional feeling on the part of the president. He did not like the Great Society."

On August 16,1971, John Dean wrote a memoir titled:

CONFIDENTIAL
SUBJECT: Dealing with our Political Enemies
... how we can use the the available federal machinery to screw
our political enemies....

1689

EXHIBIT No. 48

August 16, 1971

CONFIDENTIAL

MEMORANDUM

SUBJECT: Dealing with our Political Enemies

This memorandum addresses the matter of how we can maximize
the fact of our incumbency in dealing with persons known to be
active in their opposition to our Administration. Stated a bit
more bluntly -- how we can use the available federal machinery
to screw our political enemies.

After reviewing this matter with a number of persons possessed
of expertise in the field, I have concluded that we do not need an
elaborate mechanism or game plan, rather we need a good project
coordinator and full support for the project. In brief, the system
would work as follows:

    -- Key members of the staff (e.g., Colson, Dent Flanigan,
       Buchanan) should be requested to inform us as to who
       they feel we should be giving a hard time.

    -- The project coordinator should then determine what
       sorts of dealings these individuals have with the
       federal government and how we can best screw them
       (e.g., grant availability, federal contracts, litigation,
       prosecution, etc.).

    -- The project coordinator then should have access to
       and the full support of the top officials of the agency
       or department in proceeding to deal with the individual.

11

1690

I have learned that there have been many efforts in the past to take such actions, but they have ultimately failed -- in most cases -- because of lack of support at the top. Of all those I have discussed this matter with, Lyn Nofziger appears the most knowledgeable and most interested. If Lyn had support he would enjoy undertaking this activity as the project coordinator. You are aware of some of Lyn's successes in the field, but he feels that he can only employ limited efforts because there is a lack of support.

As a next step, I would recommend that we develop a small list of names -- not more than ten -- as our targets for concentration. Request that Lyn "do a job" on them and if he finds he is getting cut off by a department or agency, that he inform us and we evaluate what is necessary to proceed. I feel it is important that we keep our targets limited for several reasons: (1) a low visibility of the project is imperative; (2) it will be easier to accomplish something real if we don't over expand our efforts; and (3) we can learn more about how to operate such an activity if we start small and build.

Approve _____

Disapprove _____

Comment _____

In *Blind Ambition.* Dean writes, about the list:

(Charles) Colson, whose office had prepared it, defended himself with a statement that the list was nothing more than a compilation of names of people to be banned from White House functions. That much was true, but it was also true that (H.R., "Bob") Haldeman has selected some twenty people from the list who had incurred the President's special wrath. These people had been targeted for IRS audits and other government harassment, but no action had been taken, as far as I know.

Two lists would eventually grow to *over 700 names.* It had grown large enough to include supporters and staffers of George McGovern, many journalists, all black members of Congress, NFL quarterback Joe Namath, actress, singer, dancer and comedian Carol Charming.

And actor Paul Newman. He said, "My single highest honor was being No. 19 on Nixon's enemies list."

The White House political opponents project operated from 1969 to 1972. The opponents were perceived to be largely liberal and they also were believed to oppose his efforts to undermine the O.E.O. and thwart or impede his presidency.

2   John Dean, excerpt, Senate Hearing Transcript

On June 26, 1973, John Dean testified in a Senate hearing and revealed the existence of an enemies list. In his testimony, Dean said:

> I might also add that in my possession is a rather, very much down the line to what you are talking about, is a memorandum that was requested by me to prepare a means to attack the enemies of the White House.
>
> There was also maintained what was called an enemies list, which was rather extensive and continually updated.

Following a question by Senator Lowell Weicker, Dean made the documents available to the Senate committee.

1073

Mr. DEAN. The White House has made an arrangement whereby I can go to my files, but I must say it is a rather awkward arrangement. There are some five file cabinets that are all safes and there is no desk in the room to work and I must work under the supervision of a Secret Service agent and there is no place to sit down with any comfort in writing, so it is a little difficult to get in there and do anything.

Hopefully, if I were to do that, we can make arrangements so I can get in and spend the time that would be necessary to go through the files.

The other thing is, of course, I have to do this all by handwriting, because I am not allowed to make any copies of anything in my files.

Senator WEICKER. I see.

Just briefly—and this will end my questioning, and I apologize to the committee for taking so much time, but it is a subject that I confess I don't have every last bit of information on. It is a difficult thing to piece together, but I think it is a very important part of the story. I think it has become clear this afternoon that another step has been taken, another step further along the road from testimony that Mr. McCord gave, whereupon he was receiving information from the Internal Security Division; another step wherein, at least insofar as the structure of the plan of 1970, which included bugging, breaking in, burglary and the like, and the mechanics and the administration was concerned, that the first step was taken; and also, that even though that particular unit did not involve itself in any illegal activities, certainly the security arms of the U.S. Government were in various instances which you have cited utilized for purposes not intended.

Would that be a fair summation of what we are talking about?

Mr. DEAN. I am not quite sure of the end of your summation there. I wonder if you could repeat. You said that security arms were used——

Senator WEICKER. That is correct. Even though the IEC itself did not engage in any illegal activities, do you consider the matters that you have spoken of, whether it be an FBI investigation of an individual or an IRS audit, to be legal and proper activities by those security arms?

Mr. DEAN. As I say, I don't know of the IEC itself preparing political material.

Senator WEICKER. I understand.

Mr. DEAN. I do, of course, know and as I have submitted in documents, other agencies were involved in seeking politically embarrassing information on individuals who were thought to be the enemies of the White House.

I might also add that in my possession is a rather, very much down the line to what you are talking about, is a memorandum that was requested by me to prepare a means to attack the enemies of the White House.

There was also maintained what was called an enemies list, which was rather extensive and continually being updated.

Senator WEICKER. I am not going to ask who was on it. I am afraid you might answer.

I wonder, are these documents in the possession of the committee?

The next day the public became fully aware of the list. That day, June 17, 1973, CBS reporter Daniel Schorr got a copy of the enemies list and began to read it during a broadcast. It was then that he learned — on live television—that he himself was on the list.

3 The Enemies List revealed

By December, 1973, the Internal Revenue replied to the charges that the Nixon administration wanted to use the I.R.S. for political harassment and persecution (and to deflect I.R.S. investigations into Nixon's friends).

In a report titled "Investigation Into Certain Charges of the Use of the Internal Revenue Service for Political Purposes," a title which sounded like it originated in the age of Dickens, the I.R.S. hit back.

One page 1, The I.R.S. report summarized the Nixon administration's prior efforts, including testimony by John Dean on July 23, 1973:

> Dean testified that during 1971 and 1972 the White House staff operated a "Political Enemies Project." As part of the planning for the project, Dean wrote a confidential memorandum to H.R. Haldeman, John Ehrlichman, and other members of the White House staff on the subject of "how we can use the available federal machinery to screw our political enemies." The memo stated that "there have been many efforts in the past to take such actions, but they have ultimately failed— in most cases — because of lack of support at the top." In the memo, Dean recommended that the White House staff develop a list of less than ten names, as their targets for concentration.

Less than ten names.

... recommended less than ten names.

Soon Nixon administrator Charles Colson and his staff compiled a list of approximately 216 names (Appendix List #1) and independently — perhaps John Dean and/or George T. Bell or others — compiled another list (Appendix List # 2, following) — of approximately 556.

With perhaps some duplications and some errors to be resolved, the lists still totaled approximately 772 names.

R. Haldeman subsequently suggested that tax audits be conducted on certain individuals; John Dean stated that in almost all cases, that was ignored.

And, in something of an understatement, Dean said that the "Internal Revenue Service was not 'politically responsive' to the Nixon White House," and that the administration had been "unable to obtain information in the possession of the IRS regarding our political enemies."

Dean later conferred with Johnnie Walters — then I.R.S. Commissioner — and that Walters warned that further work in this area would be "inviting disaster." Walters sealed the lists and put them in an office safe — and subsequently resigned as I.R.S. Commissioner — no reason for his resignation given in the I.R.S. Report. Then ...

Internal Revenue Service commissioner Donald C. Alexander refused to launch I.R.S. audits of people on the enemies lists.

Additionally, the White House staff wanted to be kept informed about any I.R.S. investigations on people favorable to the president, as he did not want to be embarrassed by a tax case or cases involving individuals that he had personal or profession contacts with.

Requests had been made not to harass or otherwise bear down too hard on (tax) cases involving "friends."

One case, "of a prominent 'enemy' involved a gift of papers and tapes where it appears quite possible that one of the papers and tapes may relate to a period of time after the effective date of the 1969 code amendment which in effect terminated the allowance of such, deduction."

Nixon himself would later get into into substantial tax problems by wrongly valuing his papers donated.

In May 1, 1974, *The New York Times* reported that Nixon had a back tax bill of $467,000., for taxes and interest for the years 1969-1972 and that he had had paid "most of" the amount due.

He owed that amount after for a ruling by the I.R.S. that disallowed his $576,000. tax write-off for the donation of his Vice-Presidential papers to the National Archives.

The article in *The Times*, indicated it would take all of Nixon's assets and borrowed sums to pay back the complete tax bill.

The entire December, 1973 Internal Revenue Service report follows.

93d Congress } COMMITTEE PRINT
1st Session }

INVESTIGATION INTO CERTAIN CHARGES OF THE USE OF THE INTERNAL REVENUE SERVICE FOR POLITICAL PURPOSES

———

PREPARED FOR THE

JOINT COMMITTEE ON INTERNAL REVENUE TAXATION

BY ITS STAFF

DECEMBER 20, 1973

U.S. GOVERNMENT PRINTING OFFICE

WASHINGTON : 1973

25-908

JCS 37-73

CONGRESS OF THE UNITED STATES

JOINT COMMITTEE ON INTERNAL REVENUE TAXATION

HOUSE	SENATE
WILBUR D. MILLS, Arkansas, Chairman	RUSSELL B. LONG, Louisiana, Vice Chairman
AL ULLMAN, Oregon	
JAMES A. BURKE, Massachusetts	HERMAN E. TALMADGE, Georgia
HERMAN T. SCHNEEBELI, Pennsylvania	VANCE R. HARTKE, Indiana
HAROLD R. COLLIER, Illinois	WALLACE F. BENNETT, Utah
	CARL T. CURTIS, Nebraska

LAURENCE N. WOODWORTH, *Chief of Staff*

LINCOLN ARNOLD, *Deputy Chief of Staff*

(II)

LETTER OF TRANSMITTAL

CONGRESS OF THE UNITED STATES,
JOINT COMMITTEE ON INTERNAL REVENUE TAXATION,
Washington, D.C., December 20, 1973.

Hon. WILBUR D. MILLS, *Chairman,* and
Hon. RUSSELL B. LONG, *Vice Chairman,*
Joint Committee on Internal Revenue Taxation,
U.S. Congress, Washington, D.C.

DEAR MESSRS. CHAIRMEN: In its meeting on June 28, 1973, the Joint Committee on Internal Revenue Taxation instructed its staff to investigate charges that the Nixon administration used the Internal Revenue Service in its enforcement of the Internal Rvenue tax laws, for partisan political purposes.

This document reports the results of the staff investigation which deal with the treatment by the Internal Revenue Service of several hundred individuals whose names appeared on two lists of political opponents made up by the White House staff. Also, it deals to some extent with the cases of people who allegedly received favorable tax treatment because of actions taken by people in the White House.

In the case of so-called extremist individuals and extremist organizations the staff has not yet had access to the complete files in these cases. As a result, it was possible in this report to deal only to a limited extent with the allegedly extremist individuals and not at all with the extremist organizations.

This report was prepared in large part from the examination of the Internal Revenue Service's files and records and from interviews with IRS personnel. In some cases the staff also carried on independent investigations outside the Internal Revenue Service. In addition, as is noted in the report, the staff with the approval of the committee has asked the Internal Revenue Service to review a limited number of cases where the staff is not completely satisfied or the facts are not clear. The staff will again consider these cases after obtaining the further comments of the Internal Revenue Service.

Sincerely yours,

LAURENCE N. WOODWORTH,
Chief of Staff.

(III)

I. ORIGINS OF THE JOINT COMMITTEE INVESTIGATION

On June 25, 1973, John W. Dean, III, began testifying under oath before the Senate Select Committee on Presidential Campaign Activities. He made several allegations that individuals in the White House attempted to use the Internal Revenue Service for partisan political purposes. Dean alleged that he was asked to stimulate audits on several "political opponents" of the White House and to "do something" about audits that were being performed on friends of President Nixon who felt that they were being harassed by the IRS. In addition, Dean revealed the existence of a special group within the Internal Revenue Service to collect information about extremist individuals and organizations. Since Dean's testimony, there have been several newspaper articles making similar accusations about the IRS.

Under section 8022 of the Internal Revenue Code, it is the duty of the Joint Committee on Internal Revenue Taxation to investigate the administration of internal revenue taxes by the Internal Revenue Service. Therefore, following Dean's testimony before the Senate Watergate Committee, the Joint Committee met on June 28, 1973, and instructed its staff to conduct an investigation to determine whether individuals in the Nixon Administration used the Internal Revenue Service, in its enforcement of the tax laws, for any partisan political purposes.

DEAN'S CHARGES

Dean testified that during 1971 and 1972 the White House staff operated a "Political Enemies Project." As a part of the planning for the project, Dean wrote a confidential memorandum to H. R. Haldeman, John Ehrlichman, and other members of the White House staff on the subject of "how we can use the available federal machinery to screw our political enemies." The memo stated that "there have been many efforts in the past to take such actions, but they have ultimately failed—in most cases—because of lack of support at the top." In the memo, Dean recommended that the White House staff develop a list of less than ten names as their targets for concentration.[1]

The staff working on the Political Enemies Project compiled and continually updated lists of political opponents of the White House. One such list, which Dean stated was sent to him from someone on Charles Colson's staff, contained 205 names and was apparently an updated version (as of June 1971) of the opponents list. Smaller lists of high-priority opponents were prepared by Dean and by George T. Bell, another member of the White House staff. With duplications, these lists of political opponents contained 213 names. Dean also showed the Senate Watergate Committee a section of a White House news summary with a note from Lawrence Higby, H. R. Haldeman's

[1] See hearings before the Senate Select Committee on Presidential Campaign Activities, *Watergate and Related Activities, Phase I: Watergate Investigation,* 93rd Congress, 1st Session, book 4, pp. 1349–50, 1498–99, 1689–90.

assistant, to Dean indicating that the Treasurer of the Democratic National Committee, Robert Strauss, should be on the opponents list.[2]

The exhibits accompanying Dean's testimony include several other lists of individuals which apparently were the raw material from which the people involved in the Political Enemies Project constructed their lists of political opponents. These lists included people involved with the Joint Fall Peace Fund, the National Committee for the Impeachment of the President, a salute to Victor Reuther sponsored by the Americans for Democratic Action, and the Corporate Executives Committee for Peace; people who were large contributors to the Democrats in the 1968 Presidential Campaign; Muskie contributors in the 1972 campaign; people who participated in the National Labor for Peace Organization; and people on the McGovern campaign staff.[3]

Dean did not indicate that any systematic use was made of these various lists of political opponents. However, he did state that H. R. Haldeman had requested that Dean initiate tax audits on certain individuals and that Charles Colson requested that a tax audit be begun on Harold Gibbons of the Teamsters Union. Dean testified that in all but one case he ignored these requests.[4]

The exception was in the case of Robert W. Greene, the author of an article on C. G. Rebozo appearing in *Newsday* newspaper. Dean testified that he "got instructions that one of the authors of that article should have some problems." Dean expressed his reluctance to call Johnnie Walters, the Commission of Internal Revenue, on this matter. John Caulfield, who was on Dean's staff, however, told him that he "had friends in the Internal Revenue Service" and "was able to accomplish an audit on the individual" by sending an anonymous informant's letter.[5]

Dean stated in his testimony that the Internal Revenue Service was not "politically responsive" to the Nixon White House. A memorandum written by him and submitted as part of the record in the hearings stated that the administration had been "unable to obtain information in the possession of the IRS regarding our political enemies" and had been "unable to stimulate the audits of persons who should (sic) be audited." The memo indicates that Dean thought that this reluctance of people in the IRS to cooperate in this respect was a result of the domination of the "monstrous" IRS bureauracy by Democrats. This so-called political unresponsiveness was, according to Dean, of concern to President Nixon. During a September 15, 1972, meeting with Dean, the President allegedly expressed annoyance with the political unresponsiveness of the IRS, and said that after the 1972 election the administration would appoint people who would be responsive to White House requirements into agencies like the IRS.[6]

In sum, Dean's testimony indicated that there was considerable interest among individuals in the White House, including the President, in using the Internal Revenue Service to make life difficult for the political opponents of the Nixon Administration, but that Dean knew of only one case where a politically motivated tax audit actually occurred—the case of the *Newsday* reporter.

[2] *Ibid.*, book 3, p. 1073; book 4, pp. 1408–10, 1529, 1693–99, 1713–24.
[3] *Ibid.*, book 4, pp. 1700, 1705–11, 1726–53.
[4] *Ibid.*, book 4, pp. 1349, 1447, 1480, 1498, 1686.
[5] *Ibid.*, book 8, p. 1072; book 4, 1480, 1530.
[6] *Ibid.*, book 3, p. 958; book 4, pp. 1479–81, 1499, 1535, 1682–5.

Dean also testified that the White House staff tried to secure special treatment for various friends of President Nixon when they were being investigated by the IRS. He stated, "I was told to do something about these audits that were being performed on two friends of the President's. They felt that they were being harassed and the like." He cited another case in which he was told to "do something" about an audit being undertaken on someone quite close to the President. Dean stated that in this second case he checked with the Justice Department about the status of the individual in question and was told that the man was in serious trouble. Dean stated that he did nothing except keep up to date on the status of the case.[7]

Dean also mentioned a third case regarding a friend of the President about whom H. R. Haldeman wrote a note saying that he had taken care of the problem.

Dean stated that he received "a number of requests from various members of the White House staff to see if tax exemptions and alteration of the tax status could be removed from various charitable foundations and the like that were producing material that was felt hostile to the administration or to their leaders, who were taking positions that were hostile to the administration." He said that on occasion he checked these organizations out, concluded that their activities were proper under the provisions of the Internal Revenue Code, and did nothing about these cases.[8]

Dean also showed the Senate Watergate Committee several memoranda indicating that the Internal Revenue Service maintained a Special Service Group (later renamed the Special Service Staff) to monitor the activities of extremist organizations. The memos, authored by Tom Charles Huston on the White House staff, indicated that the White House had considerable interest in this Special Service Staff, but was not satisfied with the progress being made by it in monitoring ideological organizations.[9]

Enemies List Turned Over to the Internal Revenue Service

In a Joint Committee staff interview with Johnnie Walters, former Commissioner of Internal Revenue, Walters indicated that at a meeting with Dean (at 2:30 p.m. in Suite 106 of the Executive Office Building) on September 11, 1972, he received a list (referred to subsequently as enemies list 2). Apparently, at the conference he was informed that John Ehrlichman had asked that a list of this type be made up to see what type of information could be developed concerning the people on the list. The notes that Walters maintained on this conference indicate that Dean had not been asked by the President to have the IRS work done and that he did not know whether the President had asked directly that any of this work be done. In the conference, Dean apparently expressed the hope that the IRS could pick up material with respect to people on the list and could do so easily in a manner which would "not cause ripples." It was stated that Dean was not yet (the word "yet" in the notes is underlined) under pressure with respect to this information.

---

[7] *Ibid.*, book 4, p. 1530, 1558–59.
[8] *Ibid.*, book 4, pp. 1461–62, 1531.
[9] *Ibid.*, book 3, pp. 1838–45.

25

Walters' notes indicate that he advised Dean that he would discuss the matter with the Secretary of the Treasury. The notes further indicate that the matter was discussed with the Secretary on September 13 and that he directed that Walters "do nothing." Walters stated that the Secretary glanced briefly at only a few pages of the list. A second note indicates that on September 25, 1972, Dean called to ask what progress had been made on the list. The note indicates that Walters told Dean that he had discussed the matter with Secretary Shultz and that so far no progress had been made in actually checking the list. Walters advised Dean again that any checking, as he had previously suggested, would be inviting disaster. He agreed, however, to reconsider the matter again with Secretary Shultz and recall Dean. However, he informed the Joint Committee staff that he did not reconsider the matter.

Walters has indicated that he sealed the list of names and locked it in his safe in the Commissioner's office. He indicated that no one had looked at the list other than the Secretary and he. He stated further that he did not furnish any name or names from the list to anyone, nor did he request any IRS employee or official to take any action with reference to the list. He said, "with absolutely no reservation, the IRS never took any action with respect to this list." He noted that he had sealed the list the last time on May 21, 1973, at which time he cleared his files at the IRS, having resigned as Commissioner.

OTHER ALLEGATIONS CONCERNING THE INTERNAL REVENUE SERVICE

Since Dean's testimony, several newspaper articles have appeared alleging either politically motivated audits against political enemies of the White House or favoritism towards White House friends.

Columnist Tom Braden wrote a column stating that he had been audited by the IRS for the years 1969, 1970, and 1971. He wrote that he had no evidence that anyone in the White House wanted to give him a hard time but that he assumed the audits resulted from his being a White House enemy.

Columnists Jack Anderson and Les Whitten alleged that the IRS "made life miserable for Democratic National Chairman Larry O'Brien" and was moving against his successor, Robert Strauss. Anderson also reported the results of a poll taken by the American Civil Liberties Union indicating that, of the 95 White House enemies responding, 28 percent reported tax audits.[1c] Educator George Fischer of Chicago, according to Anderson, complained that he had been audited every year since 1969.

At a party given for the White House enemies in New York, philanthropist Stewart R. Mott claimed to be the victim of a "politically inspired investigation" of his taxes.

[1c] The Joint Committee Staff has asked for but not yet been able to see the details as to the ACLU poll.

II. NATURE OF THE JOINT COMMITTEE STAFF INVESTIGATION

The Joint Committee staff investigation dealt with in this report basically tries to answer three questions:

1. Did the White House Political Opponents Project have any effect on the way the Internal Revenue Service handled the tax cases of individuals?

2. Did people receive any favorable treatment from the Internal Revenue Service in tax matters because they had friends in the White House?

3. To what extent did the Special Service Staff cause individuals to be treated differently than normal because of their political views or activities?

The Joint Committee staff investigation was carried on under two different procedures. First, the staff interviewed a series of persons presently or formerly associated with the Internal Revenue Service to obtain some idea of whether and, if so, to what extent there was political influence in the administration of the internal revenue tax laws. Second, the staff examined the Internal Revenue Service's files insofar as they related to the several hundred persons listed as political opponents of the White House and also to a much shorter list of alleged friends of the White House. In addition, to the extent possible, the staff also examined files on several dozen so-called extremist individuals who were investigated by the Special Service Staff.

The staff wanted to examine the Special Service Staff's files and made an official request to the Internal Revenue Service to do so. The IRS expressed its willingness to have the staff make such an examination but, because there was FBI material in these files, indicated that it was necessary to obtain approval from the FBI before these files could be examined. A request was made of the FBI to permit the staff to examine the files (with FBI representatives present, if that was their desire). This was requested both in writing and in a personal interview with a representative of the FBI. The staff was told that this matter would have to be passed upon by the Attorney general but no reply as yet has been received. The Commissioner of Internal Revenue also wrote a letter to the FBI requesting that the staff be permitted to examine these files, but he also has received nothing in reply but an acknowledgement of his letter. At the time this report went to press a call from the Justice Department suggested that access to these files might in the near future be made available to the Joint Committee staff on a limited basis.

The files examined in connection with the several hundred political opponents included the tax returns filed, various computer-generated documents indicating whether a tax return was computer-selected for audit consideration, revenue agents' reports and work papers of audits, and so-called "sensitive case reports". In the case of the friends, much the same types of documents were examined.

The report which follows deals only with the staff findings with respect to the enemies lists, to the friends and, to the limited extent information could be obtained, the so-called extremist individuals investigated by the Special Service Staff. This report deals with the material gained through the interviews only to the extent this bears directly on matters relating to the enemies lists or to friends.

The staff believes that the report which follows is an accurate reflection of what was contained in the Internal Revenue Service's files. While it is, of course, possible that materials might have been modified or documents removed from the files before their examination by the Joint Committee staff, the staff found no evidence of this. Furthermore, any attempt to do this on any significant basis would probably have led to internal inconsistencies in the data which remained in the files and which the staff examined.

III. INTERNAL REVENUE SERVICE AUDIT SELECTION TECHNIQUES

During the years when the White House political opponents project was operating (1969 to 1972), the Internal Revenue Service used several techniques to determine which individual income tax returns should be screened by agents for possible audit.

The principal system used, known for 1968 returns as the "Standard" system, and for subsequent years known as the "Discriminant Function" (DIF) system, is wholly computerized. Under both the Standard and the DIF systems, the IRS attempts to identify those individual line items (for example, specific deductions or income items) on a tax return, the presence of which indicates that an audit of that return is likely to yield additional tax revenue. Computerized techniques are used to determine which returns contain the most of these specific items and thus have the most audit potential. (Under the DIF system the IRS uses a statistical technique known as discriminant analysis.) The number of these returns going out to a District Office for screening possible audit depends on the amount of auditing time available in the district.

The second major type of audit selection system used by the Internal Revenue Service, known in different years as the "Special" or "Automatic" selection system, is also computerized. Under this system, all return data are run through a computer to determine if the returns meet certain criteria (for example, a certain level of adjusted gross income or a certain level of unallowable deductions). All returns which meet any of these criteria are automatically sent to District Offices for screening for audit in that year. The specific criteria used to trigger automatic selection of a return vary from year to year.

A third computerized selection system is the Taxpayer Compliance Measurement Program (TCMP). Under the TCMP, the IRS selects one out of every one thousand returns and subjects these returns to a comprehensive audit. The sample is a random one within each income class; however, the sampling rate is higher in those income classes in which the IRS has historically found greater noncompliance. The data generated by these audits are then used in various research projects, including the computation of the DIF formulas.

Finally, some returns are manually selected for screening. Manual selection can occur for a variety of different reasons. Many returns are manually selected because they are related to other returns which were selected for audit. For example, partners in a business may have their returns screened as a result of an audit of any one partner, and a taxpayer's return in one year may be screened in connection with an audit of a prior or subsequent year's return. When audits of trusts or businesses lead to adjustments that should be carried through to individuals' tax returns, these returns are audited so that the changes can be made. Other returns are manually selected as a result of information from intelligence activities, news reports or informants' letters, or in connection with an IRS investigation of specific economic activities in a local area. The IRS routinely screens for audit the tax returns of people involved in criminal investigations. It also routinely screens tax returns of people who request a refund or who want to carry back an investment credit or a net operating loss.

Once a return is manually selected for screening, it will in most cases be given a full audit only after the person selecting the return examines it and determines that the return has significant audit potential. If he finds little audit potential, the IRS does not contact the taxpayer. Returns that are selected for audit consideration through the computerized DIF and Automatic systems are sent to the IRS District Office in which the taxpayer resides. At that point, the return is examined by a classifying officer of the District Office, who similarly determines whether the return has significant audit potential. If he finds little audit potential, the District Office sends the return back, and no taxpayer contact is made. The returns believed by the classifying officer to have high audit potential are assigned to revenue agents. The agents then screen the returns a second time and audit as many as they can, starting with those they think have the highest audit potential. Returns selected through the TCMP do not go through a screening process, but are automatically audited.

IV. INVESTIGATION OF INTERNAL REVENUE SERVICE FILES ON WHITE HOUSE POLITICAL OPPONENTS

The Joint Committee staff has examined the Internal Revenue Service's files on over 700 individuals who appeared on various lists of political opponents made up in the White House. List 1 consists of the 216 individuals mentioned as political opponents of the White House in John Dean's testimony before the Senate Watergate Committee.[1] The Joint Committee staff has no evidence that this list ever went to the IRS. Nevertheless, the staff examined the returns in these cases in the same manner as in the case of the returns of people whose names were given to the IRS. List 2 consists of 490 individuals whose names were given by Dean to IRS Commissioner Johnnie Walters in

[1] Dean presented three lists of political opponents to the Senate Watergate Committee, consisting of 20, 16, and 205 names. There are substantial overlaps, and the lists include 213 different individuals. In addition, Dean presented a note from Lawrence Higby stating that Democratic National Committee Treasurer Robert Strauss should be added to the list of White House political opponents. In the body of his testimony, Dean indicated that John Caulfield arranged to have a reporter from *Newsday* newspaper audited, and the staff also added to the opponents list two people affiliated with *Newsday* who participated in the article about C. G. Rebozo that occasioned Dean's interest. These are the 216 individuals on list 1.

1972.[2] For list 1, the Joint Committee staff investigation applied to individual income tax returns filed for the years 1968 to 1971. For the second list, however, the investigation was confined to returns filed for the years 1970 and 1971 unless a return for one of those years was audited, in which case the investigation was extended to one or two prior or subsequent years. In most cases, returns tend to be audited one or two years after the year for which they are filed, if they are audited at all.

The staff has not looked into the cases of people on the various supplementary lists presented by Dean to the Senate Watergate Committee unless they were also on lists 1 or 2.

SUMMARY STATISTICS ON AUDITS—LIST 1

Table 1 summarizes the audit experience of the 216 individuals on list 1. Over the four-year period 1968–1971 these people could have filed a maximum of 864 returns. In five cases, however, the individual was not required to file a return in the United States either because the individual had died or did not reside in the United States. In addition, in 17 other cases no return was filed. Thus, 842 returns were filed by the individuals on list 1.

Of these 842 returns, 491, or 58.3 percent, were screened for possible audit; and 187, or 22.2 percent, were actually audited. Twelve returns were accepted as filed but referred to a State under the Federal-State Exchange Program.[3]

TABLE 1.—AUDIT EXPERIENCE OF 216 WHITE HOUSE POLITICAL OPPONENTS 1968–1971

	Number	Percent of returns filed
Not required to file a return in United States	5	
No record of filing a return and no assurance that no return was required	17	
Return filed and not selected for screening	351	41.7
Return filed and selected for screening	491	58.3
Audited	187	22.2
Referred to a State	12	1.4
Not audited after screening	292	34.7
Total possible returns	864	
Total returns filed	842	100.0

A question which naturally arises is, how does the audit experience of the 216 enemies compare with that of the population at large. The percentage of all individual income tax returns audited during fiscal years 1969 to 1972 is available by several adjusted gross income classes.

Of the 842 returns filed by the 216 enemies, 437, or 51.9 percent, had adjusted gross income (AGI)[4] over $50,000; and 387, or 46.0 percent, had AGI between $10,000 and $50,000. Only 18 returns, or 2.1 percent,

---

[2] The second list consists of 575 names. In 45 cases, the staff could not determine the identity of the individual, and there were 41 duplications (either with list 1 or internally in list 2). In one case, the staff could not decide which of two persons was on the list, so it included both of them. Thus, 490 cases were examined.

[3] The IRS has agreements for the exchange of information with all States except Texas and Nevada. Most of the referrals on both lists were to the State of New York. Under the Federal-New York State Tax Agreement, the IRS refers to the State several thousand tax returns that it has screened and not audited because of workload limitations. New York then furnishes the results of any audit it undertakes on those returns to the IRS.

[4] Adjusted gross income is income before the deduction of personal exemptions and itemized (or standard) deductions.

had AGI below $10,000. Thus, the White House political opponents were a relatively affluent group, and it is probably appropriate to compare them with the national statistics for high income people. Internal Revenue Service data show that people with adjusted gross income over $50,000 tend to be audited about 14 percent of the time.

Since 22 percent of the returns on the White House enemies list 1 were audited, they appear to have been audited significantly more frequently than random individuals with roughly the same incomes. A finer breakdown of the national statistics, however, might not show that this was true.

There are several reasons why people on the White House political opponents list might be audited more frequently than average. First, they tend to be involved in a wider range of business activities than the average person with the same income. Second, a large fraction of the political opponents in the middle income range are journalists and writers. These people tend to have large deductions for business expenses, and under the DIF formulas in use between 1968 and 1971 this tends to give them higher-than-average DIF scores for people in their income range.

Table 2 shows the reasons why the 491 returns of people on list 1 that were screened as possible candidates for audit were selected. Of these, 425, or 86.6 percent, were selected for screening under one of the three computerized systems. Two hundred and eighty-seven returns were selected under the Standard or DIF systems, 134 under the Automatic or Special systems, and 4 under the Taxpayer Compliance Measurement Program. Twenty-one returns were screened in connection with prior or subsequent year audits. Eighteen returns were picked up in relation to audits of trusts, partnerships, or corporations. Three more were screened in connection with claims or requests for refunds. Seven were screened as part of special projects (generally, Strike Forces or Joint Compliance Projects).[5] Two were referrals from the Intelligence Division. In 15 cases there was some other reason for the screening.

In the cases in which a return was computer-selected for screening, the Joint Committee staff has verified this by examining various documents that the IRS computer routinely generates when such a selec-

TABLE 2.—REASONS FOR SCREENING RETURNS FROM LIST 1

		Number	Percent
Total screened		491	100.0
Computer selected		425	86.6
Standard or DIF system	287		58.5
Automatic or special systems	134		27.3
Taxpayer Compliance Measurement Program	4		0.8
Multi-year audit		21	4.3
Related pick-up[1]		18	3.7
Claims and other requests for refunds		3	0.6
Intelligence Division referrals or requests		2	0.4
Special projects[2]		7	1.4
Other		15	3.0

[1] Returns picked up in connection with audits of other returns.
[2] Mainly Strike Forces and Joint Compliance Projects.

---

[5] Strike Forces refer to the use of the investigative resources of several Federal agencies, including the IRS, to fight organized crime. In 1972, the IRS closed 5,894 audits in connection with Strike Forces. Joint Compliance Projects are carried out by the Audit and Intelligence Divisions within each District. They are directed against any individuals in the District who engage in specific economic activities that the IRS suspects are associated with failure to comply with the tax laws.

tion is made. In the cases where a return was audited in connection with a prior or subsequent year audit, the staff has verified that the prior or subsequent year audit did indeed occur and determined why the return was selected for screening that year. In cases of related pick-ups, the staff has verified that the related trust, partnership or corporation was indeed audited. In the cases of returns in which there were claims or requests for refunds, the staff has verified that such claims were made. In the case of special projects, the staff has either traced a project to an investigation begun by some other government agency or, if it was initiated by the IRS itself, examined the project to see that it was conducted without regard to the political views or activities of the individuals under investigation. In the other cases, the staff has satisfied itself that screening was not the result of White House pressure on the IRS.

Informants' letters present special problems. Any person who wishes to have somebody audited by the IRS can try to do so by sending a convincing informant's letter. Presumably, there is no reason why somebody in the White House could not send an anonymous letter (or even a signed letter) as well. Dean testified before the Senate Watergate Committee that this is how Caulfield arranged to have the *Newsday* reporter audited. (The staff, however, did not find any informant's letters in this file.) The files on the individuals on list 1 contained 30 informants' letters on 19 people, of which 8 were anonymous. In many cases, these were the sort of crank letters that are routinely written to, and about, public figures. In no case was a return screened or audited because of such a letter. In one case, however, a letter was referred to an agent who was already auditing the subject of the letter, and the letter led to the assessment of a $365 deficiency.

Of the 187 audits, 121 had been completed by the time of the Joint Committee staff investigation. Thirty-one led to no change in tax liability; 82 to a tax increase; and 8 to a tax reduction.

SUMMARY STATISTICS ON AUDITS—LIST 2

The staff has also examined files on 1,417 returns of the 490 individuals on list 2. Table 3 summarizes the audit experience of the individuals on list 2 only for the years 1970 and 1971. In those two years the 490 individuals could have filed a maximum of 980 returns. Actually, they filed 962 returns. Of these, 569, or 59.1 percent, were selected for screening and 253, or 26.3 percent, were audited. Seven returns were referred to States under the exchange program. As was true in the case of list 1, this represents a higher percentage of cases audited than for people with high incomes generally. However, as previously pointed out, there are differences between this group and high income persons generally which may well account for the higher percentage audited.

Of the 1,417 returns examined for all years, the IRS selected a total of 999 returns for screening. Table 4 summarizes the reasons why these returns were selected. In 802 cases, or 80.3 percent of the total, the return was selected by one of the computer systems. Of these, 367 were selected under the Standard or DIF systems, 416 under the Automatic or Special systems, and 19 under the Taxpayer Compliance Measurement Program. In 17 cases, the screening was associated with a claim or request for a refund; and in 35 cases it was a result of a prior or subsequent year audit. There were 65 pick-ups related to audits of businesses or trusts. Five returns were screened because of Intelligence referrals or requests. Eleven returns were screened as the result of special projects. Sixty-four returns were screened for some other reason.

TABLE 3.—AUDIT EXPERIENCE OF 490 WHITE HOUSE POLITICAL OPPONENTS 1970 AND 1971

		Number	Percent of returns filed
Not required to file a return in 1970 or 1971		2	
No record of filing a return and no assurance that no return was required		16	
Return filed and not selected for screening		393	40.9
Return filed and selected for screening		569	59.1
Audited	253		26.3
Referred to a State	7		.7
Not audited after screening	309		32.1
Total possible returns		980	
Total returns filed		962	100.0

TABLE 4.—REASONS FOR SCREENING RETURNS FROM LIST 2

		Number	Percent
Total Screened		999	100.0
Computer selected		802	80.3
Standard or DIF system	367		36.7
Automatic or Special systems	416		41.7
Taxpayer Compliance Measurement Program	19		1.9
Multi-year audit		35	3.5
Related pickup [1]		65	6.5
Claims and other requests for refunds		17	1.7
Appellate or Intelligence Division referrals or requests		5	0.5
Special projects [1]		11	1.1
Other		64	6.4

[1] See notes to Table 2.

As with the returns from list 1, the staff has verified the reasons why each of these 999 returns on list 2 were selected for screening. It has found no evidence that any returns were screened as a result of White House pressure on the IRS.

CONDUCT OF AUDITS AND COLLECTION AND INTELLIGENCE ACTIVITIES

In addition to determining whether an individual on one of the political opponents lists was audited in a particular year, the staff has examined the revenue agents' reports and the workpapers of each audit to judge whether the audits were conducted without harassment or undue strictness. Income tax audits necessarily involve some inconvenience for the taxpayer being audited. However, the staff has found no evidence that revenue agents attempted to increase unnecessarily this inconvenience for people on the political opponents lists. In some cases, the agents were relatively strict. However, this was usually motivated by a previous lack of cooperation on the part of the taxpayer. In an equal number of cases the agents were somewhat lax. The staff has found absolutely no evidence that audits of people on the political opponents lists were on the average conducted more harshly than normal.

33

The staff has also reviewed the collection activities of the IRS concerning people on the lists. It has found no evidence that the IRS has been more vigorous in its attempts to collect unpaid taxes from political opponents of the White House than normal. Indeed, if anything, the opposite is true. Several individuals on the lists appear to pose collection problems for the IRS. The Service has been quite lenient in granting extensions to file in many cases, and has not yet attempted to collect taxes from several political opponents who have failed to file returns or even to ascertain the reasons for the failure to file.

The staff has also found no indication that the IRS was more vigorous than normal in recommending prosecution for tax violations in the cases of political opponents of the White House.

Cases of Alleged IRS Bias

The staff's investigation paid particular attention to the cases of those individuals mentioned in the press as victims of politically motivated audits. The Joint Committee staff has difficulty in discussing these cases specifically because of the problem this would present in violating the individuals' rights of confidentiality. However, in none of these cases has the staff found any evidence that the taxpayer was unfairly treated by the Internal Revenue Service because of political views or activities. If the staff were freed from restraint as to disclosure of information, it believes the information it has would indicate that these taxpayers were treated in the same manner as taxpayers generally.

In one case, it is possible to make some comments since the information involved does not come from Internal Revenue Service files. This was the case involving Robert W. Greene, a reporter for *Newsday* who had authored an article on C. G. Rebozo. In this case, Dean stated that John Caulfield had initiated an audit with an informant's letter. According to statements made by Greene, however, his return was not audited by the Internal Revenue Service but rather by New York State under the Federal/State exchange program. The staff has talked with Mr. Greene, the New York revenue agent who audited Greene's State return, and other people in the New York State Department of Taxation and, as a result, believes that his audit by New York State was unrelated to his being classified as a White House enemy.

V. INVESTIGATION OF INTERNAL REVENUE SERVICE FILES ON "FRIENDS" OF THE WHITE HOUSE

Seven individuals have been reported in the media or in testimony before the Senate Select Committee on Presidential Campaign Activities to be friends of people in the White House who allegedly received some favorable tax treatment because of actions taken by persons in the White House. In all of the 7 cases called to the staff's attention, audits were undertaken by the Internal Revenue Service. It is believed that all 7 of these were, at one time or another, listed as "sensitive case reports." Such reports are maintained on a current basis within the Internal Revenue Service for cases involving prominent persons. A listing of this type apparently has been used since the Eisenhower administration when Dana Latham was Commissioner of Internal Revenue. It has been stated that the principal purpose of this list is to keep top officials in the Internal Revenue Service informed of the status of cases in progress where problems may be raised and to assure that Service officials are not uninformed if news relative to some case appears in the press. In addition, the listing has apparently been used to inform top personnel in the Treasury outside of the Internal Revenue Service about cases being developed on prominent people. It is clear that the White House staff has been notified about cases being developed which might affect persons with whom the President may come in contact. The purpose is to insure that he is not embarrassed by a tax case which suddenly appears in the press with respect to a person with whom he has had social or official contacts.

Statements have also been made that on occasion names on the sensitive case list have been seen by those on the White House staff and that requests have been made not to harass or otherwise bear down too hard on cases involving "friends." It is clear from information available that in 2 or 3 of the cases such requests were made by White House personnel. In one case, to demonstrate that there was no harassment, a special study was made by the Internal Revenue Service to show that the returns of others in the same industry were given at least as much attention as was the return of the taxpayer in question. In another case, it is clear that there was a communication from the Commissioner of Internal Revenue to a District Director and to the agent working on the return regarding a "friend's" return. On the other hand, in the case of one "friend" an indictment has been obtained, and in another case the audit is continuing. In another situation, the Government did not prosecute a case involving a prominent "friend." Questions may be raised as to whether this was the appropriate action.

In reviewing the returns, the staff finds it difficult to "second-guess" the agents who were actually performing the audits. The staff believes that in three cases there are substantial questions about decisions made by governmental agencies about friends of the White House, but the staff does not have evidence that there was any pressure involved. With the approval of the committee, the staff has requested the IRS to reexamine these cases and to present analyses showing why it believes further action should, or should not, be taken.

While the staff is not as yet satisfied as to some of the cases involving "friends," the staff also believes that a number of "enemies" either were not audited when the staff believes they should have been or were audited too leniently. In some of the "enemies" cases, errors were clearly made where more careful examination of the returns would have disclosed an underpayment of tax. In one "enemies" case, an individual subtracted his minimum tax payment from his regular tax rather than adding it. In another case involving a prominent "enemy" of the administration, the Service recomputed the tax due and erred in not adding his self-employment tax to the total tax due. Another case of a prominent "enemy" involves a gift of papers and tapes where it appears quite possible that some of the papers and tapes may relate to a period of time after the effective date of the 1969 code amendment which in effect terminated the allowance of such a deduction.

Still another "enemies" case involves an individual with a large income where harassment was alleged. In fact, there was no audit in this case by the IRS although it appears that the screening should have resulted in an audit based upon items appearing on the face of the return. In another such case, there is a serious question as to how expenses for food for a particular diet can be classified as travel expenses.

Finally, there are sixteen cases (involving eleven individuals) on enemies list 2 where no return was filed at all. On list 1 there were 17 such cases (involving 8 individuals). In some of these cases, the individuals involved apparently are students who may well owe no tax. Other cases, however, involve prominent individuals where it is difficult to believe that no tax is owed.

In addition to requesting the Internal Revenue Service to review some of the cases involving the "friends," the staff, with the approval of the Joint Committee, has submitted to the Internal Revenue Service a request to audit a number of the returns of the "enemies" and to investigate the cases where no returns at all were filed.

In summary, there are cases on both the friends and enemies lists in which people who probably should have been audited were not audited, in which audits were not done adequately, or in which returns were not filed and no collection activity has been undertaken. Therefore, the Joint Committee staff does not conclude, although it cannot foreclose, that the instances of lenient audits of White House friends were the result of White House pressure on the IRS. As a result, the staff, with the approval of the Joint Committee, has requested further reports from the IRS with respect to certain friends' cases, as well as in the cases of certain enemies.

VI. THE SPECIAL SERVICE STAFF

HISTORY

In 1969 the Permanent Subcommittee on Investigations of the Senate Committee on Government Operations held extensive hearings on civil disorders. A certain Jean Powell, a former member of the Black Panther Party, testified under oath that the party received between $50,000 and $100,000 each month and that most of this income flowed directly to the officers of the party. It was noted that the Black Panthers had never filed Federal tax returns and had never been audited by the Internal Revenue Service. This revelation caused Senator Karl Mundt, the ranking Republican on the Committee, to comment on the "special treatment" being given to the party and its members. Other evidence was presented indicating that certain extremist organizations and individuals were evading taxes.[1]

Shortly thereafter and presumably in response to the evidence presented at the Senate hearings, the IRS created a special unit to gather information about the finances of so-called extremist organizations and individuals. This unit, the Activist Organizations Committee, began operating in August 1969. In 1970, the IRS renamed it the Special Service Group, and subsequently its name was changed to the Special Service Staff ("SSS").

---

[1] See hearings of the Permanent Subcommittee on Investigations of the Senate Committee on Government Operations, *Riots, Civil, and Criminal Disorders,* 92nd Congress, 1st Session, p. 3788.

At some stage, the SSS appears to have shifted its emphasis from extremists *per se* to organizations and individuals who preached noncompliance with the tax laws.

Several congressional committees cooperated with the SSS by providing information to it about extremist organizations and individuals. These included the Permanent Subcommittee on Investigations of the Senate Committee on Government Operations, the House Committee on Internal Security, and the Subcommittee on Foundations of the House Select Small Business Committee.

While the existence of the SSS was known to these congressional committees, its existence was not announced to the general public until April 1972, when it was mentioned in the Internal Revenue Manual. However, the description contained there did not mention the fact that the SSS was concerned only with allegedly extremist or (later) tax resistance and protest organizations. The IRS did not release a more complete description of the function of the SSS until June 1973, after Dean's testimony.

In August 1973, the IRS decided that financial information about tax resisters and protesters could be gathered adequately by the regular divisions of the Service, and it abolished the SSS.

FUNCTION

The function of the SSS was to gather information on the finances and activities of extremist organizations and individuals, both right and left, and make this information, along with recommendations about what to do with it, available to the appropriate division of the IRS. The Joint Committee staff has not been allowed access to the files of the SSS; however, the IRS states that the main sources of this information were congressional committees, the FBI, the Justice Department, the Defense Department, other branches of the IRS, and various publications. The SSS referred information to the Audit, Collection, Intelligence, and Alcohol, Tobacco and Firearms Divisions. (The Joint Committee staff has not as yet investigated the Alcohol, Tobacco and Firearms Division in this particular regard; however, it is presently conducting a study into their activities in coordination with the General Accounting Office.) The SSS did not engage in either audit or collection activity itself, nor did it make recommendations about criminal prosecutions. Its recommendations were rather that a certain tax return should be examined by the Audit Division or that the Collection Division should investigate a certain individual who has not filed an income tax return but appears to have income in excess of the filing requirement.

The SSS collected a large amount of information. Apparently, in June 1972, there were 9,800 separate information files on 2,500 organizations and 7,300 individuals.

As of August 1972 after three years of operation, the SSS had referred 182 cases to the field. (It is not clear what fraction of these went to the Alcohol, Tobacco, and Firearms Divisions.) Of these 182 cases, 103 cases had been closed. In 51 of these cases, there was no productive result. The remaining cases led to the filing of 124 tax returns with tax liabilities of $56,000 and refunds of $4,000 as well as to audit deficiencies of $50,000 on returns that had been filed. In addition, information furnished by the SSS led to the collection of

16

a Taxpayer Delinquency Account amounting to $2,600. The total revenue yield of the SSS in these three years, then, was slightly over $100,000.

THE JOINT COMMITTEE INVESTIGATION

The Joint Committee staff has examined the cases of 37 individuals about whom referrals of information were made by the SSS to either the Audit, Collection, or Intelligence Divisions. These cases included many of the prominent radicals who were active in the years 1969 to 1972 as well as several rightwingers.

The Joint Committee staff has used the same procedures and data for these individuals that it used for the White House political enemies on lists 1 and 2. In addition, the staff examined the summaries of the SSS files that the SSS prepared and sent to the Audit, Intelligence and Collection Divisions.

Clearly, the establishment of a special unit to gather and disseminate to the IRS divisions information about individuals with "extremist" political views in itself means that these individuals were selected for special attention. Some such special effort with respect to individuals who preach noncompliance with tax laws (since it is likely that they will practice it as well) may be in a somewhat different category.[2]

The Joint Committee staff, however, has found no evidence that individuals about whom referrals of information were made by the SSS to the Audit, Intelligence, and Collection Divisions were treated any more harshly by these divisions than was normal. Indeed, in some cases the IRS seems to have been more lenient than normal with prominent extremists, perhaps in order to avoid the charge that radicals were being persecuted.

Even though several of the individuals whose files were examined are chronic nonfilers, none have been prosecuted for their failure to file. The Collection Division does not appear to have made an inordinate effort to collect small amounts of tax, as it presumably would do if it wished to harass the individuals in question. In some cases, the IRS has not yet even attempted to collect unpaid taxes.

Since the staff has not as yet been allowed access to the files of the SSS, as indicated above, it has not completed its investigation of the treatment by the IRS of the organizations about whom referrals were made by the SSS.

---

[2] The prior administrations singled out some rightwing extremists for special attention by the IRS. This effort was on a much smaller scale than the recent investigation. Only tax-exempt organizations, not individuals, were examined, and the project was confined to only 22 such organizations.

APPENDIX A

ENEMIES LIST 1

(The names and addresses contained on this list are those names and addresses which were received by the committee and no attempt has been made to ascertain whether or not the names have been spelled correctly or the addresses are current.)

INDIVIDUALS

Abel, I. W. (Bernice), 3216 Apache Road, Pittsburgh, Pa.
Abernathy, Ralph (Juanita), 76 Cerro St., Atlanta.
Abzug, Bella (Mrs. Maurice), 37 Bank St., New York.
Alexander, Clifford Jr. (Adele), 512 "A" St., S.E., Washington, D.C.
Anderson, Jack (Olivia), 7300 Burdette Ct., Bethesda, Md.
Anderson, William R. (Yvonne), 2700 Virginia Ave., Washington, D.C.
Barkan, Alexander E. (Helen), 6515 E. Halbert Road, Bethesda, Md.
Barnet, Richard, 1712 Portal Drive, Washington, D.C.
Bayh, Birch (Marvella), 219 Garfield St., N.W., Washington, D.C.
Beneson, Charles B., 941 Park Ave., N.Y.C.
Bengston, Nelston, 200 E. 36th St., N.Y.C.
Bernstein, Leonard (Felica), 205 W. 57th St., 551 5th Ave., N.Y.C.
Bishop, Jim (Elinor), Golden Isles, 442 Tamarind Dr., Hallandale, Florida.
Balke, Eugene Cakson (Valina), Country Club Rd., New Cahaan, Conn.
Bok, Derek Curtis (Sissela), 33 Elmwood Ave., Cambridge, Mass.
Brademas, Stephen John, 750 LeLand Ave., South Bend, Ind.
Braden, Thomas, 101 E. Melrose, Chevy Chase, Md.; 825 Dolly Madison Parkway, McLean, Va.
Brewster, Kingman Jr. (Mary) 43 Hillhouse Ave., New Haven, Conn.
Brown, Holmes.
Bruckner, D. J. R., Suite 730–1700, Penn Ave., Washington, D.C.
Bundy, McGeorge (Mary), 1040 5th Avenue, N.Y.C.
Buttenweiser, Benjamin, c/o Kuhn Leob & Co., 40 Wall Street, N.Y.
Calkins, Hugh (Ann), 1750 Union Commerce Bldg., Cleveland, Ohio.
Chait, Lawrence G. (Sylvia), 32 Linwood Dr., Valley Stream, N.Y.
Chanes, Ernest R., 34 W. 9th St., N.Y.C.; 213 E. 27th St., N.Y.C.
Channing, Carol (Mrs. Charles F. Lowe), 14921 Ventura Blvd. #312, Sherman Oaks, Calif.
Childs, Marquis, 2703 Dunbarton St., Washington, D.C.
Chisholm, Shirley, 1028 St. Johns Place, Brooklyn, N.Y.
Chomsky, Avram Noam (Carol Doris), 15 Suzanne Road, Lexington, Md.
Clark, Ramsey (Georgia), 3 W. 12 St., N.Y.C.
Clay, William (Carol A.), 633 Whittingham Dr., Silver Springs, Md.
Clifford, Clark (McAdams), 9421 Rockville Pk., Bethesda, Md.
Collins, George W. (Cardiss), 1438 So. Ridgeway Ave., Chicago, Ill.
Conyers, John Jr., 19970 Cantebery Rd., Detroit, Mich.
Cosby, Bill (Camille), 1900 Ave. of the Stars, Suite 1900, Los Angeles, C.A.
Culter, Lloyd (Norton), (Louise), 5215 Chamberlin Ave., Chevy Chase, Md.
Dane, Maxwell (Belle), 650 Park Ave., N.Y.C.
Davidoff, Sidney, 250 East 73 St., New York, New York
Deakin, James (Doris), 6406 Whittier Court, Bethesda, Md.
DeBakey, Michail Ellis (Diane), 5323 Cherokee St., Houston, Texas.
Dellums, Ronald (Leola), 1749 N. Portal Dr., N.W. Oakland, Calif.
Diggs, Charles C., Jr. (Janet), Washington, D.C.; Detroit, Mich.
Dogole, S. Harrison, Presidential Apt., Phila., Pa.
Doyle, James S., 6401 Tone Drive, Bethesda, Md.
Drinan, Robert Frederick, 140 Commonwealth Ave., Newton, Mass.
Dudman, Richard B. (Helen), 3409 Newark St., N.W., Washington, D.C.

(17)

Duscha, Julius (Carl), (Priscilla), 3421 Raymond St., Chevy Chase, Md.
Dyson, Charles Henry (Margaret), 24 Tomriaus oad, Scarsdale, N.Y.
Eaton, William (James), (Marilynn), 1106 Trinity Drive, Alexandria, Va.
Eisner, Norman 100 Overlook Terrace, N.Y.C.
Ellsberg, Daniel.
Evans, Rowland Jr. (Katherine), 3125 O St., N.W., Washington, D.C.
Feld, Bernard T. (Eliza), 42 Arlington St., Cambridge, Mass.
Feller, Karl, 3106 Manning Ave., Cincinnati, Ohio.
Finch, Charles Baker (Angela), 167 82nd St., New York City, N.Y.
Fischer, George Drennen, 260 E. Chestnut, Apt. 4301, Chicago, Ill.
Fonda, Jane (Mrs. Roger Vadim), c/o Frusch, 120 E. 56th St., Room 1010, New
    York, New York.
Frazier, George, 81 Upland Road, Winthrop, Mass.
Friedman, Saul (Evelyn), 11503 Bucknelle Drive, Silver Spring, Md.
Fritchey, Clayton (Naomi), 2100 Massachusetts Ave., NW., Washington, D.C.
Fulbright, James William (Elizabeth), Fayetteville, Ark. (1000 Shrewsbury).
Galbraith, J. Kenneth (Catherine), 30 Frances Ave., Cambridge, Mass.
Gardner, John (Aida), 5325 Kenwood Ave., Chevy Chase, Md.
Gelb, Lesley, 2405 Elba Court, Alexandria, Va.
Gibbons, Harold J., 4466 West Pine, St. Louis, Mo.
Goldfinger, Nathaniel (Clara), 306 Hamilton Ave., Silver Spring, Md.
Goodell, Charles, 12 Elmark Road, Bronxville, N.Y.
Goodman, Julian (Betty Davis), 15 Greystone Road, Larchmont, N.Y.
Gottlieb, Sanford (Gladys), 11102 Brandywine, Kensington, Md.
Gregory, Dick (Lillian), 1451 E. 55th St., Chicago, Ill.
Greene, Robert.
Guest, Raymond R.
Grospiron, A. F. (Etta), 2777 South Eastern Way, Colorado.
Guinan, Matthew, 3890 Sedgwich Ave., Bronx, New York.
Guthman, Edwin (Joanne), 1436 N. Capri Dr., Pacific Palisades, Calif.
Halperin, Morton, 8215 Stone Terrace Dr., Bethesda, Md.
Hammil, Pete, 1771 Troy Avenue, Brooklyn, N.Y.
Harrington, Michael (1) (Stephanie), 1182 Broadway, New York City, N.Y.
Harris, Fred R. (LaDonna), 1104 Waverly Way, McLean, Va.
Harris, Patricia (Roberts) (Mrs. Wm. Beasley Harris), 1742 Holly St., N.W.,
    Washington, D.C.
Harris, Sydney, 401 N. Wabash, Chicago, Ill.
Hawkins, Augustus Freeman (Peggy), 125 N. Carolina Ave., S.E., Washington,
    D.C.; (Los Angeles, Calif.)
Healy, Robert Edward (1), (Jeanette), 17 Cavanaugh Road, Boston, Mass.
Heineman, Frank (7), 6 Eve Lane, Rye, N.Y.
Heller, Walter (Wolfgang) (5) (Emily), 2203 Farwell St., St. Paul, Minn.
Hemenway, Russell D. (2), 8711 Second Ave., Rye, N.Y.
Hickel, Walter (Joseph), P.O. Box 1700, Anchorage, Alaska.
Hillman, George, 11 5th Ave., N.Y.C.
Hines, William Jr. (Ethel), 152 G St., S.W., Washington, D.C.
Hughes, Harold (Eva), 813 Carrie Court, McLean, Va.
Jennings, Paul (Dorothy), 1126 16th St., N.W., Washington, D.C.
Kalb, Marvin (Madeleine), c/o Stanley Goldstein & Co., 135 E. 55th St., N.Y.C.
Karnow, Stanley (Annette), 1515 L Street, N.W., Washington, D.C.
Kastenmeier, Robert William, (Dorothy), 300 No. Water Street, Watertown,
    Wisc.
Kenin, Herman D., 14 Northfield Drive, Westport, Conn.
Kennedy, Edward Moore (Virginia Joan), 3 Charles River Square, Boston, Mass.
Kimelman, Henry L. (Charlotte), Virgin Islands.
Kirkland, Joseph Lane (Edith), 1200 Old Georgetown Road, Rockville, Md.
Knap, Ted (Thaddeus), 1429 Woodacre Drive, McLean, Va.
Knoll, Erwin, 4202 River Road, Washington, D.C.
Kondracke, Morton, 3812 Van Ness St., N.W., Washington, D.C.
Kraft, Joseph (Polly), 3021 N Street, N.W., Washington, D.C.
Laird, James.
Lambert, Samuel M. (Juanita), 3144 Oliver St., N.W., Washington, D.C.
Land, Edwin (Helen), 163 Brattle St., Cambridge, Mass.
Lapin, Raymond H. (Mary), 86 San Carlos Ave., Sausalito, Calif.
Laventhol, David A. (Ester), 22 Bayview Ave., Port Washington, N.Y.
Lerner, Max (Edna), 445 E. 84th St., New York, N.Y.
Levey, Stanley (Nan), 611 G. St., S.E., Washington, D.C.

Lewis, Flora, 11912 Old Bridge Rd., Rockville, Md.

Ley, Herbert L. Jr. (Doris), 9209 Friars Rd., Bethesda, Md.

Lichenstein, Bertram, 14 E. 75th St., N.Y.C. (Dilton Ltd. 290 Ave. of the Americas).

Lindsay, John V. (Mary), Gracie Mansion, New York, N.Y.

Loeser, Hans F., 78 Washington Ave., Cambridge, Mass.

Loory, Stuart, 5546 29th St., N.W., Washington, D.C.

Lowenstein, Allard K. (Jennifer), 163 Lindell Blvd., Long Beach, N.Y.

McCarthy, Eugene J. (Abigail), 301 First St., N.E., Washington, D.C.

McGee, Vincent Jr., 501 W. 122 St., N.Y.C.

McGovern, George, Mitchell, South Dakota; 3020 University Terrace, Washington, D.C.

McGrory, Mary, 2710 Macomb St., Washington, D.C.

McKee, Gerald, 2 Park Ave., N.Y.C.

McNamara, Robert S. (Margaret), 2412 Tracy Place, Washington, D.C.

McQueen, Steve T. (Neile), 9134 Sunset Blvd., Los Angeles, C.A.

Macy, John Williams Jr. (Joyce H.), 1127 Langley Lane, McLean, Va.; Office-888 16th St., N.W., Washington, D.C.

Manealoff, William, 210 Central Park South, N.Y.

Manning, Robert Joseph (Margaret M.), 191 Commonwealth Ave., Boston, Mass.

Mankiewicz, Frank (Holly), 5408 Duvall Dr., Washington, D.C.

Meselson, Matthew Stanley (Sarah), 11 Moon Hill Road, Lexington, Mass.

Metcalfe, Ralph H. (Madelynne), 4530 So. Michigan Ave., Chicago, Ill.

Miller, Joseph Irwin (Xerria R.), 2760 Highland Way, Columbus, Ohio.

Millstone, James (Pat), 6985 Princeton, St. Louis, Mo.

Milstein, Paul, 76 Birchall Drive, Scarsdale, N.Y.

Mitchell, Parren J., 951 Brooks Lane, Baltimore, Md.; 1228 Longworth Office Bldg.

Mondale, Walter F. (Joan), Minneapolis, Minn., 3421 Lowell St., Washington, D.C.

Morgenthau, Hans J. (Irma), 19 E. 80th St., New York, N.Y.

Morrisett, Lloyd N. (Mary F.), Cedarlawn Road, Irvington, N.Y.

Mott, Stewart Rawlings, 515 Madison Ave., New York, N.Y.

Munro, S. Sterling Jr., 711 Lamberton Drive, Silver Spring, Md.

Muskie, Edmund S. (Jane), Main Street, Waterville, Maine.

Namath, Joe William, 1604 Ross Hill, Beaver Falls, Pa.

Nelson, Gaylord Anton (Carrie Lee), 618 Bordner Drive, Madison, Wisc.

Newman, Paul (Joanne W.), c/o E. Traubner, 1800 Central Park East, Los Angeles, Calif.

Newton, Hughie, 1200 Lakeshore, Oakland, Calif.

Niles, Henry Edward (Mary C.), 307 Tuscany Road, Baltimore, Md.

Nix, Robert N. C. (Ethel L.), 2139 N. 22nd St., Philadelphia, Pa.

Nolan, Martin, 6400 31st Place, Washington, D.C.

O'Neal, Frederick (Charlotte), 41 Convent Ave., N.Y.C.

O'Neal, Thomas, 4209 Tuscany Court, Baltimore, Md. (Died 3 years ago).

Osburne, John (Gertrude), 2917 O. St., N.W., Washington, D.C.

Palmer, Charles, Silver Spring, Md.

Palmieri, Victor H. (Martha C.), 116 Malibu Colony Road, Malibu, Calif.

Patman, Wright (wife deceased), 1205 Main St., Texarkana, Tex.

Peck, Gregory, 9171 Wilshire Blvd., Suite 420 Beverly Hills, Calif.

Phillips, Lawrence S., 219 E. 69 St., New York, N.Y.

Picker, Arnold (Nettie R.), 200 Golden Beach Drive, Golden Beach, Florida.

Pierson, John, 1604 32nd St., Washington, D.C.

Pirie, Robert S.

Pollock, William (Anna M.), Ofc.-99 University Pl., New York, N.Y.

Potofsky, Jacob S. (wife deceased), 19 E. 88th St., New York, N.Y.

Prochnau, William W., 3808 Pleasant Ridge Rd., Annadale, Va.

Proximire, William (Ellen H.), 4613 E. Buckeye Road, Madison, Wisc.

Randall, Tony, 5636 LaMirada, Hollywood, Calif.

Rangel, Charles Bernard (Alma C.), 4807 Colorado Ave., N.W., Washington, D.C.

Raskin, Marcus (Barbara), 1820 Wyoming Ave., N.W., Washington, D.C.

Reston, James Barrett (Sarah J.), 3124 Woodley Road, N.W., Washington, D.C.

Rhodes, Joseph Jr., Harvard University, Boston, Mass.

Roosa, Robert Vincent (Ruth G.), 59 Wall St., New York, N.Y.

Rose, David, 39 Oxford Road, Scarsdale, N.Y.

20

Rosenfield, Joseph Frankel (Dannil), 700 Hubbel Bldg., Des Moines, Iowa.
Roth, Julian, 166 E. 63rd St. (850 3rd Ave.), N.Y.C.
Rovere, Richard Halworth (Eleanor A.), 108 Montgomery St., Rhinebeck, N.Y.
Rowan, Carl Thomas (Vivian L.), 3116 Fessenden St., N.W., Washington, D.C.
Rowen, Henry Stanislaus (Beverly G.), 2 Wisteria Way, Atherton, Calif.
Ruder, William (Helen B.), Beverly Road, Rye, N.Y.
Rustin, Bayard, 340 W. 28th St., N.Y., N.Y.
Samuelson, Paul Anthony (Marion C.), c/o North East Merchants Bank, 28 State Street, Boston, Mass.
Scharer, Seymore, 6 Romala Drive, Kings Point, N.Y.
Schlesinger, Arthur Meier Jr. (Marion C.), Ofc. 33 W. 42nd Street, New York, N.Y.
Schorr, Daniel Louis, c/o N.S. Bienstock, 850 7th Avenue, N.Y.C.
Selden, David S. (Bernice), 7102 Rebecca Drive, Alexandria, Va.
Semer, Milton Philip (Charlene), Southdown Farm, Great Falls, Va.
Sherrill, Robert, 617 N. Carolina Ave., S.E., Washington, D.C.
Shriver, Robert Sargent Jr. (Eunice M.), c/o T. J. Walsh, Room 3021, 200 Park Avenue, N.Y., N.Y.
Slaner, Alfred Philip (Luella B.), 10 Normandy Lane, Scarsdale, N.Y.
Sonnabend, Roger Philip (Elsa G.) Odell Road, Sandouner, N.H.
Sorensen, Theodore (Camilla), 345 Park Ave., New York, New York.
Stark, Ray (Frances B.), 2 Beekman Pl., New York, N.Y.
Stein, Howard (Janet), 767 Fifth Ave., New York, N.Y.
Stokes, Louis (Jeanette F.) 12600 Shaker Blvd., Cleveland, Ohio.
Stone, Jeremy, 264 A "G" St. S.E., Washington, D.C.
Strauss, Robert S. (Helen).
Streisand, Barbra (Mrs. Elliott Gould), c/o Hecht Brayer & Grill, 1501 Broadway, N.Y.
Sweig, Morton, 983 Park Ave., N.Y.C., N.Y.
Talbot, George H., 417 Hermitage Road, Charlotte, N.C.
Taylor, Arthur Duane (Roberta), 375 Rosemary Lane, Ruddy, Calif.
Tishman, Alan V. & Margaret, 131 Briar Brae Road, Stamford, Conn.
Tucker, Lem, 175 W. 13th St., N.Y.C.
Unna, Warren W., 121 6th St., N.E., Washington, D.C.
Valenti, Jack Joseph, 1st Street, N.W., Washington, D.C.
Van Horne, Harriet (Mrs. William Lowe), N.Y.C.
Vanocur, Sander (Edith), c/o Jules Lefkowitz & Co., 1350 Ave. of the Americas, N.Y.C.
Viorst, Milton, 3432 Ashly Terrace, N.W., Washington, D.C.
Wallace, George Corley (Cornelius), 3465 Norman Bride Road, Montgomery, Ala.
Wallach, Ira David (Miriam), 5 Sherbrooke Road, Scarsdale, N.Y.
Warnke, Paul Culliton (Jean F.) 5037 Garfield St., N.W., Washington, D.C.
Watson, Thomas J. Jr. (Olive F.), Meadowcroft Lane, Greenwich, Conn.
Watts, William, 3100 45th St., N.W., Washington, D.C.
Wechsler, James A. (Nancy F.), 185 West End Ave., N.Y., N.Y.
Weissman, George (Mildred S.), 81 Manursing Way, Rye, N.Y.
Weller, Ralph Albert, 39 E. 67th St., N.Y.C.
Wicker, Thomas Grey (Neva J.), 3333 Cleveland Ave., N.W., Washington, D.C.
Wiesner, Jerome Bert (Laya W.), 61 Shattuck Road, Watertown, Mass.
Wiley, George, 1608 Q St., N.W., Washington, D.C.
Wills, Garry, 624 Overbrook Road, Anselott, Md.
Woodcock, Leonard, 1300 Lafayette, Detroit, Mich.
Wurf, Jerry (Mildred Kiefer), 3220 Cleveland Ave., N.W., Washington, D.C.

APPENDIX B

ENEMIES LIST 2

(The names and addresses contained on this list are those names and addresses which were received by the committee and no attempt has been made to ascertain whether or not the names have been spelled correctly or the addresses are current.)

M/M Richard Abrons, 10 Rigene Road, Harrison, N.Y. 10528.
Thomas Boylston Adams, Concord Road, Lincoln, Mass. 01773.
Isadore Adelman, 1035 Summit Drive, Beverly Hills, Calif.
Julius Ochs Adler, 50 E. 77th St., New York, N.Y. 10021.
Dr. Sheldon Adler, 474 Duquesne Dr., Pittsburgh, Pa. 15243.
Archibald Alexander, 744 Broad St., Newark, N.J. 07102.
Henry Alker, 512 Wyckoff Rd., Ithaca, N.Y.
Bruce Allen, 5411 S. Harper Ave., Chicago, Ill. 60615.
Herb Alpert, 1416 North LaBrea Ave., Hollywood, Calif.
Judith H. Alpert, Box 452, Princeton, N.J.
Frank Altschul, 730 Fifth Ave., New York, N.Y. 10019.
William R. Anixter, 279 Moraine Road, Highland Park, Ill.
Joseph Antonow, 111 East Wacker Drive, Chicago, Ill.
Paul S. Armington, 3031 Macomb St., Washington, D.C. 20008.
Mrs. Elaine Attias, 605 N. Bedford Drive, Beverly Hills, Calif.
Milton S. Axelrad, 687 Driftwood Lane, Northbrook, Ill.
M/M John Axtell, 10 Lincoln Road, Scarsdale, N.Y.
Mildred E. Barad, (No Address).
Irving Barr, 11 5th Ave., New York, N.Y. 10003.
Jim Barrett, 7621 N.W. 34th., Okalhoma City, Okla. 73008.
Robert Batinovich, 100 Flying Cloud Island, Foster City Calif. 94406.
Doris Z. Bato, Cognewaugh Road, Cos Cob, Conn. 06807.
Dr./Mrs. Bernard Batt, 31 Livingston Road, Sharon, Mass.
Dr./Mrs. Theodore B. Bayles, 94 Summer St., Weston, Mass. 02193.
Mrs. J. (Helen) Beardsley, 7336 Monte Vista, La Jolla, Calif. 92037.
John M. Behr, 10820 Vicenza Way, Los Angeles, Calif.
Charles Benton, 585 Ingleside Place, Evanston, Ill.
Marjorie Benton, 585 Ingleside Place, Evanston, Ill. 60201.
Polly Bergen, Los Angeles, Calif.
Jerome Berger, 35 Ridgemoor Drive, Clayton, Mo. 63105
Louise Berman, 6 West 77th St., New York, N.Y.
Nahum A. Bernstein, 295 Madison Ave., New York, N.Y. 10017
Peter L. Bernstein, 767 Fifth Ave., New York, N.Y. 10022
Harold Berry, 19330 Stratford, Detroit, Mich.
Harold & Vivian Berry, 16300 N. Park Dr., Apt. 1517, Southfield, Mich. 48075.
Mrs. Carly Billings, P.O. Box 1014, Sag Harbor, N.Y. 11963.
Eugene C. Blake, 256 Country Club Road, New Canaan, Conn.
Louis C. Blau, 9777 Wilshire Blvd., Beverly Hills, Calif. 90212.
Leonard Block, 257 Cornelison Ave., Jersey City, N.J. 07302.
Elizabeth Blossom, 56 Linnaean St., Cambridge. Mass.
Mrs. Frances Boehm, 1 Willow Lane, Hewlett Harbor, N.Y. 11557.
M/M Robert Boehm, 1 Willow Lane, Hewlett Harbor, N.Y. 11557.
Edward G. Boettiger, Dunham Pond Road, Storrs, Conn. 06268.
Alva T. Bonda, 11 Bratenahl Place, Suite 14E, Bratenahl, Ohio; and 1700 Investment Plaza, Cleveland, Ohio 44114.
Joel Bonda, Investment Plaza, Cleveland, Ohio 44114.
Lou Bonda, Investment Plaza, Cleveland, Ohio 44114.
Richard Borow, 1800 Ave. of the Stars, Los Angeles, Calif. 90067.
M/M Constantine & Elizabeth Boukas, P.O. Box 116, Dunnigan, Calif. 97102.

((21)

Michael Brande, 1360 N. Sandburg, Chicago, Ill.
M/M Irwin H. Braun, 546 N. Cliffwood Ave., Los Angeles, Calif.
Gerald Breslauer, 3306 Barbydell Drive, Los Angeles, Calif.
John Briscoe, Silent Meadow Farm, Lakeville, Conn. 06039.
Robert L. Brock, 1153 Stratford Road, Topeka, Kan.
Earl Brockelsby, Box 2063, Rapid City, S. Dakota.
George Brockway, 63 Brevoot Rd., Chappaqua, N.Y.
Edward R. Broida, 2222 Corinth Ave., Los Angeles, Calif. 90064.
John Brown, 5811 Orton Road, Louisville, Ky.
M/M Lester R. Brown, 8716 Preston Place, Chevy Chase, Md. 20015.
Robert W. Brown, 371 Noco Lane, Menlo Park, Calif.
M/M Roger Brown, 3249 O Street, N.W., Washington, D.C. 20007.
M/M Thomas Buckner, 445 Boynton, Berkeley, Calif. 94707.
Stimson Bullitt, 1125 Harvard E., Seattle, Washington 98102.
Carter Burden, 305 E. 79th St., New York, N.Y.
Walter Burke, Winding Lane, Greenwich, Conn.
Michael Butler, Los Angeles, California.
Michael Butler, Oak Brook, Ill.
Alexander and Luisa Calder, Roxbury, Conn. 06783.
William D. Carleboch, 1112 Hardscrabble Rd., Chappaqua, N.Y. 10514.
M/M Robert Carlson, 495 Prospect Blvd., Pasadena, Calif.
William H. Carter, 2222 Ave. of the Stars, Los Angeles, Calif. 90067.
Jerome Cassidy, 3515 Wilshire Blvd., Los Angeles, Calif.
Raymond Cerf, 1000 Sunset Drive, Lawrence, Kan.
Mrs. David (Joan R.) Challinor, 3117 Hawthorne St., N.W., Washington, D.C. 20008.
Tertius Chandler, 2720 Elmwood Ave., Berkeley, Calif.
R. B. Chaote, 3508 Macomb St., N.W., Washington, D.C. 20016.
Ann Chapman, 1026 Maxine, Flint, Mich.
Edwin Child, 73 W. Cedar St., Boston, Mass. 02114.
John C. Childs, 1020 Cromwell Bridge Rd., Baltimore, Md. 21204.
Ellis Chingos, 7707 North Federal Highway, Boca Raton, Fla. 33432.
Jane Ann Choate, Hudson House, Ardsley-on-Hudson, N.Y.
Willard Chotiner, 10501 Wyton Dr., Los Angeles, Calif.
Blair Clark, 229 E. 48th St., N.Y., N.Y.
Mrs. Alice Erdman Cleveland, Bonnytop, Tamworth, N.H. 03886.
Michael Coburn, 26 Witherspoon Lane, Princeton, N.J. 08540.
Isadore M. Cohen, 1290 Ave. of the Americas, New York, N.Y.
Lionel Cohen, P.O. Box 884, Gary, Indiana 46401.
M/M Ronald B. Cohen, 3509 Severn Road, Cleveland Heights, Ohio 44118.
Saul and Amy Cohen, 203 Hommocks Rd., Larchmont, N.Y.
A. Cohn, 1440 North Lake Shore Drive, Chicago, Ill.
Catherine W. Coleman, 101 West Monument St., Baltimore, Md. 21201.
Louis L. Colen, 2727 Krim Drive, Los Angeles, Calif.
Ms. Lucinda C. Collins, 19 W. 12th St., New York, N.Y. 10011.
M/M Randolph P. Compton, 53 Brookby Rd., Scarsdale, N.Y. 10583.
Edward T. Cone, 18 College Road West, Princeton, N.J. 08540.
P. F. Conrad, 29328 North Bay Road, Palos Verdes, Calif.
M/M Andrew D. Cook, 48 Academy Rd., Apt. 6, Westmount, P.Q., Canada.
Tim Cooney, 201 East 21 St., New York, N.Y.
Edward T. Corre, 18 College Road West, Princeton, N.J.
Phyllis Cox, 88 Garden St., Cambridge, Mass.
William H. Crocker, 3333 P Street, N.W., Washington, D.C.
P. McEvoy Cromwell, 710 Circle Road, Ruxton, Md.
Ruth Cromwell, 710 Circle Road, Ruxton, Md.
Priscilla Cunningham, 160 East 72nd St., New York, N.Y. 10021.
Dorothy V. Dalton, 1130 Short Rd., Kalamazoo, Mich.
Eugene S. Daniell, Jr., Franklin National Bank Bldg., Franklin, N.H.
Joan K. Davidson (No address).
Alan S. Davis, 37 West 12th St., New York, N.Y.
Ed G. Davis, 319 Harden Burg, Demarest, N.J. 07627.
Irving Davis, 1300 Midvale, Los Angeles, Calif. 90024.
Stewart W. Davis, Innstrasse 16, 8 Munich 80, Germany.
Mark B. Dayton, 900 Old Long Lake Rd., Wayzata, Minn.
Lucy F. DeAngulo, 2845 Buena Vista Way, Berkeley, Calif. 94708.
Morris Dees, Rolling Hills Ranch, Matthews, Ala. 36052; or P.O. Box 2087, Montgomery, Alabama.

Mrs. June Oppen Degnan, Ames Ave. & Shady Lane, P.O. Box 1036, Ross, Calif. 94957.
Lawrence Deutsch, 1800 W. Magnolia Blvd., Burbank, Calif.
Adrian W. DeWind, 345 Park Ave., New York, N.Y. 10021.
Carl Djerassi, 127 Cresta Vista, Portola Valley, Calif.
Henri G. Doll, 18 East 78th St., New York, N.Y.
Inez W. Dries, 61 Superior Drive, Campbell, Calif.
Martha Ward Dudley, 2942 Macomb St., N.W., Washington, D.C. 20008.
Angier Biddle Duke, 47 Chester Square, London, SW 1, United Kingdom.
Abe Dunn, 3100 West Alabama, Suite 203, Houston, Tex. 77520.
Cornelius Dutcher, 7712 Moonridge Place, La Jolla, Calif. 92037.
Cornellus & Barbara Dutcher, 7617 Convoy, San Diego, Calif.
M/M Oscar Dystel, 666 Fifth Ave., New York, N.Y. 10019.
Norman Eisner, 16 Shady Brook Rd., Great Neck, N.Y.
Richard A. Eisner, 280 Park Ave., New York, N.Y. 10016.
Donald F. Eldridge, 167 Isabella Ave., Atherton, Calif. 94025.
Lawrence Ellman, 1 W. 72nd St., New York, N.Y.
Helen W. Ellsworth, Salisbury, Conn. 06068.
Victor Elmaleh, 860 United Nations Plaza, New York, N.Y. 10017.
James S. Ely, 170 Gregory Hill Rd., Rochester, N.Y.
Richard Emerson, Wells Hill, Lakeville, Conn. 06039.
George G. Emert, 9512 Singleton Drive, Bethesda, Md. 20034.
Beatrice Blair Epstein, 292 Ambassador Dr., Rochester, N.Y. 14610.
Michael C. Erlanger, Redding, Conn. 06875.
Dominick Etcheverry, 41 E. 10th St., New York, N.Y. 10011.
Ralph Ettlinger, Jr., 1370 Lincoln Ave., So., Highland Park, Ill. 60035.
S. Sanford Ezralow, 9556 Sherwood Forest, Beverly Hills, Calif. 90210.
Max Factor, 336 S. Hudson, Los Angeles, Calif.
M/M Gary & E. Familian, 1011 Cove Way, Beverly Hills, Calif.; or 9134 Sunset Blvd., Los Angeles, Calif.
Mary Dupont Faulkner, c/o State Street & Trust, Boston, Mass.; and 255 Goddard Ave., Brookline, Mass.
S. Ferry, 1572 Massachusetts Ave., Cambridge, Mass. 02138.
Stanley Feuer, 23140 Marisposa De Oro, Malibu, Calif.
Martin D. Fife, 180 Madison Avenue, New York, N.Y.
John Fisher, 123 Part St., Buffalo, N.Y.
Mark H. Fleischman, 36 East 38th St., New York, N.Y. 10016.
Moe Foner, Drug Hospital Union.
M/M J. Malcomb Forbes, 133 Coolidge Hill, Cambridge, Mass.
Orville Forte, Jr., 40 Nobscott Rd., Weston, Mass.
M/M Stanley A. Frankel, 161 E. 42nd St., New York, N.Y.
John French, 100 Wall Street, New York, N.Y. 10005.
Michel Fribourg, Two Broadway, New York, N.Y.
Jules L. Furth, 2450 Lakeview Ave., Chicago, Ill.
Mrs. Helen Fuson, 325 College Ave., Richmond, Indiana 47374.
Andrew Gagarin, Gallos Lane, Litchfield, Conn. 06758.
John B. Gage, 683 Santa Barbara Rd., Berkeley, Calif.
Margaret Gage, 11769 Sunset Blvd., Los Angeles, Calif.
Mrs. Elizabeth Galande, Dickson Mill, Greene Village, N.J.
John Kenneth Galbraith, Harvard University, 207 Littaner, Cambridge, Mass.
Florence Gardner, Chicken Valley Rd., Locust Valley, N.Y.
Samuel Gary, 1776 Lincoln St., Denver, Colo.
Jerome Ginzberg, 25 Hutchinson Pkwy., Lynbrook, N.Y.
J. W. Gitt (Gritt(?)), Hanover, Pa.
M/M(?) J. W. Gitt, Pinehurst, North Carolina, 28374.
Ralph Gleason, 10th and Parker, Berkeley, Calif.
M/M Martin L. Gleich, 2210 4th Ave., San Diego, Calif. 92101.
Alan Glen, 5454 Wisconsin Ave., NW., Chevy Chase, Md. 20015.
Seth M. Glickenhaus, 30 Broad St., New York, N.Y. 10004.
Robert & Susan Glickman, 29 Oxford Rd., Scarsdale, N.Y. 10503.
Michael J. Goldberg, 15366 Longbow Drive, Sherman Oak, Calif.
Margaret S. Goheen, Princeton University, Princeton, N.J.
Dr. Orville J. Golub, 359 Veteran Ave., Los Angeles, Calif.
Elinor Goodspeed, 1230 13th St., NW., Washington, D.C.
Howard Gottlieb, 1000 Lake Shore Blvd., Evanston, Ill. 60202.
Isabella Grandin, 301 Berkley St., Boston, Mass. 02116.
Edith B. Greenberg, 10591 Rocca Way, Los Angeles, Calif.

Kenneth L. Greif, 4000 N. Charles St., Baltimore, Md.
I. A. Grodzins, 5737 S. Blackstone, Chicago, Ill.
George Gund, Gund Ranches, Lee, Nevada 89801.
Richard S. Gunther, 707 North Bedford Drive, Beverly Hills, Calif.
John H. Gutfreund, Salomon Bros. & Hutzler, (Address unknown).
Richard Tod Gutknecht, 19890 Lures Lane, Huntington Beach, Calif. 92646.
Gene Hackman, 9171 Wilshire Blvd., Los Angeles, Calif.
Hugh Hamill, 384 Milne St., Philadelphia, Pa. 19144.
Victor G. Hanson, 15929 W. Seven Mile Rd., Detroit, Mich. 48235.
Irving B. Harris, First National Plaza, Chicago, Ill. 60670.
Anne B. Harrison, 3556 Macomb St., NW., Washington, D.C. 20016.
Carmen Harschaw, 417 S. Hill St., #434, Los Angeles, Calif. 90013.
Nan A. Harvie, 3317 Paty Drive, Honolulu, Hawaii 96822.
Henry Waldron Havemeyer, 350 Fifth Ave., New York, N.Y. 10001.
Mr. Heckler, 201 East 42nd St., New York, N.Y.
Hugh M. Hefner, 919 North Michigan Ave., Chicago, Ill.
William Hegarty, 448 North St., Greenwich, Conn.
Fred Heim, 2973 Passmore Drive, Los Angeles, Calif.
Frank Heineman, 120 East 34th St., New York, N.Y.
Alfred E. Heller, 121 Woodland, Kentfield, Calif. 94904.
Clarence S. Heller, 244 California St., San Francisco, Calif.
Ruth B. Heller, 121 Woodland, Kentfield, Calif. 94904.
M/M Paul & Ruth Henning, 4250 Navajo St., North Hollywood, Calif.
R. Allen Hermes, R.D. #2, West Redding, Conn. 06896.
M/M Alexander P. Hixon, Jr., 5443 Palisade Ave., Bronx, N.Y. 10471.
Harrison Hoblitzelle, 16 Gray Gardens West, Cambridge, Mass. 02138.
Harold Hochschild, Blue Mt. Lake, N.Y. 12812.
John P. Hodgkin, 515 Madison Ave., New York, N.Y. 10021.
LeRoy E. Hoffberger, 900 Garrett Bldg., Baltimore, Md. 21209.
Janet Hoffheimer, 198 Green Hills Rd., Cincinnati, Ohio.
Joseph Hofheimer, 2 Great Jones St., New York, N.Y. 10012.
Alice A. Hoge, 63 East Bellevue, Chicago, Ill.
David L. Hollander, 2518 Talbot Rd., Baltimore, Md. 21216.
Louis Honig, 3555 Pacific Ave., San Francisco, Calif.
Tim Horan, Wunderman, Ricotta & Kline, 575 Madison Ave., New York, N.Y. 10022.
Raymond Horne, 725 Bryson St., Youngstown, Ohio 44502.
Alice A. Howe, 63 East Bellevue, Chicago, Ill.
Rudolph Hurwich, Box 1030, Berkeley, Calif.
Peter Hutchinson, 221 D. Halsey, Princeton, N.J. 08540.
Raymond Iekes, 111 Alvarado, Berkeley, Calif. 94705.
James H. Inglis, 8811 Colvesville Rd., #803, Silver Spring, Md.
Jennifer L. Jacobs, 577 West Ferry, Apt. 3, Buffalo, N.Y.
Edwin Janss, Jr., 104 Thousand Oaks Blvd., Thousand Oaks, Calif. 91360.
Christopher Jencks, c/o Cambridge Trust Co., Cambridge, Mass.
Ester Johnson, R.D., Oldrick, N.J.
M/M Walter Johnson, 19641 Coral Gables, Southfield, Mich. 48075.
Alfred W. Jones, 435 E. 52nd St., New York, N.Y. 10022.
Catherine S. Jones, 2728 32nd St., N.W., Washington, D.C. 20008.
Larry Kagan, 1900 Ave. of the Stars, Los Angeles, Calif.
Albert J. Kallis, 528 N. Palm Drive, Beverly Hills, Calif.
Sheila Kamerman, 1125 Park Place, New York, N.Y.
Louis Kane, 10 Chestnut St., Boston, Mass.
Jack Kaplan, 760 Park Ave., New York, N.Y.
Frank Karelsen, 600 Park Ave., New York, N.Y.
David Karr, 47 Rue Faubourg St. Honore, Paris, France.
Samuel Katzin, 5530 S. Southshore, Chicago, Ill.
Anita Katzman, 100 Sands Point Rd., Longboat Key, Sarasota, Fla. 33577.
Don Kaufman, 3100 Mandeville Canyon Rd., Los Angeles, Calif.
M/M Elwood P. Kaufman, 148 Library Place, Princeton, N.J.
Gloria Kaufman, 3100 Mandeville Canyon Rd., Los Angeles, Calif.
Harold Keith, 93 Malibu Colony, Malibu Calif. 90265.
Dorothy Kent, San Juan, Pueblo, New Mex. 87566.
James R. Kerr, 1275 King St., Greenwich, Conn.
Jim Kerr, 10850 Wilshire Blvd., Los Angeles, Calif.
Peter Kessner, 112 W. 34th St., New York, N.Y. 10001.
Henry L. Kimelman, P.O. Box 250, St. Thomas, Virgin Islands. 00801.

Dr. & Mrs. J. J. King, 7121 W. Manchester Ave., Los Angeles, Calif.
David B. Kinney, 3636 N. 38th St., Arlington, Va. 22207.
Travis Kleefeld, 8929 Wilshire Blvd., #212, Beverly Hills, Calif. 90211.
Mrs. S. B. Knight, Box 174, Gates Mills, Ohio 44040.
Arthur J. Kobacker, 3172 Homewood Ave., Steubenville, Ohio 43952.
Harvey L. Koizim, 145 Main St., Westport, Conn. 06880.
Gilman Kraft, 401 St. Cloud Rd., Los Angeles, Calif.
Herbert Kronish, 1345 6th Ave., New York, N.Y.
Violet Krum, 43 N. Housac Rd., Williamstown, Mass.
Norman Kunin, 600 Old Country Road, Garden City, N.Y. 11530.
Mrs. Joseph Lachowicz, 1042 N. 5th Ave., Tucson, Ariz. 85705.
Lou Lamberty, 301 South 51st Ave., Omaha, Nebr.
M/M Corliss Lamont, 315 W. 106th St., New York, N.Y. 10025.
Mrs. Helen Lamont, 315 W. 106th St., New York, N.Y. 10025.
Roy Lamson, 68 Francis Ave., Cambridge, Mass. 02138.
Burt Lancaster (No address).
Peter Lake, 10005 Reevesbury Dr., Beverly Hills, Calif.
Bert Lane, 224 South June St., Los Angeles, Calif. 90004.
Theodore V. Lane, 1330 De Soto, Canoga Park, Calif.
Frank E. Laplin, Princeton, N.J.
H. Irgens Larsen, 10 Frog Rock Rd., Armonk, N.Y. 10504.
Frank Lautenberg, 405 Route 3, Clifton, N.J.; or 36 Stonebridge Rd., Montclair, N.J.
Norman Lear, 132 S. Rodeo Drive, Beverly Hills, Calif.
Mrs. Lucy B. Lemann, 525 Park Ave., New York, N.Y.
Timothy Leonard, 1027 City Park, Columbus, Ohio.
George Leppert, 20 Leroy St., Potsman, N.Y. 13676.
M/M Albert W. Lerch, 1511 Amalfi Dr. Pacific Palisades, Calif.
Mrs. Beatrice Lerner, 300 Lillore Road, South Orange, N.J.
Alvin Levin, Old Winter St., Lincoln, Mass. 01773.
Robert A. & Kay Levin, 1411 Judson Ave., Evanston, Ill.
Abner Levine, 2 Amberly Road, Lawrence, N.Y.
Joseph E. Levine, 1301 Ave. of the Americas, New York, N.Y.
M/M Bernard Levy, 91 Chatham Road, Kensington, Conn. 06037.
Diana B. Lewis, 778 Park Ave., New York, N.Y.
M/M Peter B. Lewis, 18930 South Woodland Rd., Shaker Heights, Ohio 44122.
Robert K. Lifton, 201 E. 42nd Street, New York, N.Y.
Timothy Light, 104 Eastern Heights Dr., Itahca, N.Y.
William E. Little, Jr., 220 Fifth Avenue, New York, N.Y. 10001.
William Louis-Dreyfus, One State Street Plaza, New York, N.Y. 10004.
Dr. A. A. Lumsdaine, University of Washington, Seattle, Washington 98105.
Mrs. Frances B. McAllister, P.O. Box 1874, Flagstaff, Ariz. 86001.
Fred McConnaughey, 2230 S. Patterson Blvd., Dayton, Ohio 45409.
F. R. McConnaughey, 4385 Tam-o-Shanter Way, Kettering, Ohio 45429.
Alan McGowan, 16785 Bayview Drive, Sunset Beach, Calif.
Priscilla McMillan, 12 Hilliard St., Cambridge, Mass.
John E. Mack, 111 Beverly Road, Chestnut Hill, Mass.
Elizabeth Mackie, 98 Bayard Lane, Princeton, N.J.
Milton Maidenberg, 1100 Euclid Ave., Marion, Ind.
Lewis Manilow, 105 W. Adams St., Chicago, Ill. 60603.
Stanley Marsh, 115 W. 7th Ave., Amarillo, Texas.
Anne Martindell, 1 Battle Road, Princeton, N.J. 08450.
Priscilla Mason, 2817 N Street, N.W., Washington, D.C. 20007.
Stephanie May, Duncaster Rd., Bloomfield, Conn. 06002.
Kenneth Pray Maytag, 21 East Canon Perdido, Santa Barbara Calif.
C. W. V. Meares, 307 East 44th St., New York, N.Y. 10017.
J. J. Meeker, 4511 Ridgehaven Rd., Forth Worth, Tex.
Daniel Melcher, 228 Grove St., Montclair, N.J.
M/M Charles Merrill, 23 Commonwealth Ave., Boston, Mass. 02116.
Robert Mertens, P.O. Box 245, Woodstock, Vermont 05091.
Mrs. LuEsther T. Mertz, 860 United Nations Plaza, Apt. 30E, New York, N.Y. 10017.
Howard M. Metzenbaum, 1700 Investment Plaza, Cleveland, Ohio 44114.
Ruth Meyer, 252 Huntington St., New Haven, Conn. 06511.
Harry C. Meyerhoff, 6301 Reistertown Rd., Baltimore, Md. 21215.
Jack Meyerhoff, 5560 Collins Avenue, Miami Beach, Fla.
Robert Meyerhoff, 3209 Fallstaff Road, Baltimore, Md.

Jean Milgram, 5 Longford St., Philadelphia, Pa.
Gerlad J. Miller, 1220 Blair Mill Rd., Silver Spring, Md. 20910.
Joseph Miller, 1913 Delancey Place, Philadelphia, Pa.
M/M Marshall Miller, Gateway Towers, Apt. 20K, Pittsburgh, Pa.
M/M Richard G. Miller, Box 621, R.R. #1, Carson City, Nev. 89701.
Leon R. Miral, M.D., 4821 E. McNichols, Detroit, Mich. 48212.
Ralph Mishkin, 7130 LaPresa Drive, Los Angeles, Calif.
Robert L. Misrack, 901 S. Hill St., Los Angeles, Calif. 90015.
Stuart Moldaw, 49 Faxon Road, Atherton, Calif.
Kenneth Monfort, 1902 25th Ave., Greeley, Colo.
Jenny McKean Moore, 6619 Newark St., N.W., Washington, D.C.
Carol S. Moss, 335 S. Rimpau, Los Angeles, Calif.
M/M Jerome S. Moss, 1416 N. LaBrea Ave., Hollywood, Calif.
Stewart Mott, 515 Madison Avenue, New York, N.Y. 10022.
M/M Stuart Mudd, 734 Millbrook Lane, Haverford, Pa. 19041.
William W. Mullins, 509 S. Linden, Pittsburgh, Pa.
Eleanor E. Murdock, 301 Berkeley St., Boston, Mass. 02116.
David C. Nash, 305 E. 40th St., Apt. 5F, New York, N.Y. 10016.
Mrs. Margaret De Neufville, Thomas Road, Mendham, New Jersey 07945.
C. M. Newman, 9820 Spring, Omaha, Nebr.
Murray Newman, 8405 Indian Hills Dr., Omaha, Nebr. 68124.
Nick Newman, 9820 Spring, Omaha, Nebr.
Paul & Joanne Newman, Westport, Conn. 06880.
Frederick M. Nichols, 9454 Wilshire Blvd., Beverly Hills, Calif.
Georgia O'Keefe, Albuquerque, New Mexico
Wilfred A. Openhym, 230 Park Ave., New York, N.Y. 10017.
M/M Harold Oram, 77 Park Ave., New York, N.Y. 10016.
Albert Ornstein, 210 E. 86th Street, New York, N.Y. 10028; and Apt. M-11,
    Bldg. 2, Washington Square Village, New York, N.Y.
Moe Ostin, Warner Brothers, Burbank, Calif.
Mrs. Louise Ottinger, 150 Central Park South, New York, N.Y. 10019.
Mrs. Joan B. Overton, (No address)
Janet F. Page, 1007 Paseo de la Cuma, Santa Fe, New Mex. 87501.
Joan Palevsky, 623 S. Beverly Glen Blvd., Los Angeles, Calif. 90024.
Max Palevsky, 755 Stradella, Los Angeles, Calif. 90024.
Victor Palmieri, 107 Malibu Colony, Malibu, Calif.
Esther Parker, 177 Lake St., Sherborn, Mass.
Mrs. Grace Parr, Box 463, Taos, New Mex. 87571.
J. R. Parten, 1603 Bank of the Southwest Building, Houston, Texas.
Isaac Patch, 185 Maple St., Englewood, N.J. 07631.
Henry Pearlman, 630 Third Ave., New York, N.Y. 10017.
Edward R. Peckerman, Jr., 230 Park Ave., New York, N.Y. 10017.
Martin Peretz, Assistant Professor, Harvard University, (No address).
Harry J. Perry, PNB Building, Philadelphia, Pa.
Robert O. Peterson, 530 B St., San Diego, Calif. 92101.
Donald A. Petrie, 2500 Virginia Ave., NW., Washington, D.C.
Gifford Phillips, 825 S. Barrington Ave., Los Angeles, Calif.
M. Platov, Tannersville, N.Y. 12485.
Gene Pokorny, Rte. #2, Howells, Nebr.
A. Polland, 716 W. Arbor Drive, San Diego, Calif.
Jerry E. Poncher, 7400 Caldwell Avenue, Chicago, Ill. 60648.
Sidney L. Port, 2961 Gregory St., Chicago, Ill.
Bibb Porter, 78 E. 56th St., New York, N.Y.
Rubin Potoff, 574 E. Main St., Waterbury, Conn.
Diane S. Poucher, 303 N. Deere Park Dr., Highland Park, Ill. 60035.
M/M Charles Pratt, 242 E. 68th St., New York, N.Y. 10021.
George Pratt (George D., Jr.), Bridgewater, Conn. 06752
Mrs. Jean Wood Preston, Weston Road, Lincoln, Mass. 01773.
Julian Price II, 1776 Butler Creek Rd., Ashland, Oregon; and Box 5786, Greens-
    boro, N.C.
Bernard Rabinowitz, 2 Laurel Lane, Clifton, N.J.
Reuben Rabinowitz, 2 Laurel Lane, Clifton, N.J.
Bernard Rapoport, Box 208, Waco, Tex.
Joan Rea, 510 Park Ave., New York, N.Y.
Charles R. Reed, 402 A Deuereux, Princeton, N.J. 08540.
Walter T. Ridder, 1325 E St., NW., Washington, D.C. 20004.
Ellis Ring, 11400 Rochester Ave., Los Angeles, Calif.

M/M Joseph Robbie, 1301 NE. 100th St., Miami, Fla. 33138.
James Robbin, 740 Cordova Ave., San Diego, Calif.
Edward Hutchinson Robbins, 5303 Boxwood Court, Washington, D.C. 20016.
Bernard M. Rodin, 919 Third Ave., New York, N.Y.
M/M Richard Rogers, 2 East 61 St., New York, N.Y. 10021.
M/M Frank Roosevelt, 404 Riverside Drive, New York, N.Y. 10025.
Carl Rosen, Essex, N.Y.
Jaclyn B. Rosenberg, 1155 Shadow Hill Way, Beverly Hills, Calif.
Richard S. Rosenzweig, 1519 Euclid Ave., Marion, Indiana.
Mike Roshkind, 6464 Sunset Blvd., Los Angeles, Calif.
Stanley Rothenfeld, 19100 South Park Blvd., Shaker Heights, Ohio.
Arvin K. Rothschild, Universal Marion Bldg., Jacksonville, Fla.
Walter Rothschild Jr., 521 Fifth Ave., New York, N.Y. 10017.
James W. Rouse, 10354 Windstorm Drive, Columbia, Md.
Miles Rubin, 77 Malibu Colony, Malibu, Calif. 90265.
Mrs. Vera Rubin, 1080 Fifth Ave., New York, N.Y.
*Dr. Vera Rubin, 1028 Fifth Ave., New York, N.Y.
Madeline Russell, 3778 Washington St., San Francisco, Calif.
Edward L. Ryerson, Jr., 71 Washington Ave., Cambridge, Mass.
John D. Ryan, Northville, N.Y. 11234.
M/M Eli Sagan, 153 Dwight Place, Englewood, N.J. 07631.
Eli J. Sagan, 520 8th Ave., New York, N.Y.
Alan Sagner, 301 So. Livingston Ave., Livingston, N.J. 07039.
Alan Saks, 3840 West Fullerton Ave., Chicago, Ill.
Elizabeth M. Salett, 6 Kensington Ave., Trenton, N.J. 08618.
Richard Salomon, 870 United Nations Plaza, New York, N.Y.; and Riverbank
   Road, Stamford, Conn.
Maxwell H. Salter (and Mrs. Janet), 804 N. Linden Drive, Beverly Hills, Calif.
Edward and Rose Sanders, 509 Tuallitan Road, Los Angeles, Calif. 90049.
Stanley Sands, 2601 Woodcrest, Lincoln, Nebr.
David Sanford, 614 Pearson, Flint, Mich.
William H. Scheide, 133 Library Road, Princeton, N.J.
Fred Schiener, 18 Beverly Drive, Great Neck, N.Y. 11021.
J. L. Schiffman, 15 Exchange Place, Jersey City, N.J.
Robert Schlossberg, 3846 Virginia St., Lynwood, Calif.
Leland Schubert, 2 Bratenahl Place, Bratenahl, Ohio.
Leonard Schulman, 444 Park Ave., S., New York, N.Y.
Mrs. Milton Schulman, 737 Park Ave., New York, N.Y.
Edward L. Schuman, 4201 Cathedral N.W., Washington, D.C. 20016.
Kenneth L. Schwartz, 4280 North Hills Drive, Hollywood, Fla. 33021.
Burnell Scott, 276 N. Pleasant, Oberlin, Ohio.
Peter J. Scott, P.O. Box 388, Lyndhurst, N.J. 07071.
Marvin Shapiro, 1800 Ave. of the Stars, Los Angeles, Calif.
Betty Warner Sheinbaum, 819 San Ysidro Lane, Santa Barbara, Calif. 93103.
Stanley K. Sheinbaum, 819 San Ysidro Lane, Santa Barbara, Calif.
Ralph Shekes, 16 W. 77th St., New York, N.Y. 10024.
Malcolm Sherman, 10450 Waterfowl Terrace, Columbia, Md. 21044.
Richard Sherwood, 9606 Feather Road, Beverly Hills, Calif. 90210.
Mrs. Richard T. Shields, 812 Fifth Ave., New York, N.Y. 10021.
Emilie Helene Siebert, 310 Riverside Dr., New York, N.Y. 10024.
Jerome A. Siegel, 1175 Old White Plains Rd., Maranoneck, N.Y. 10543.
Joan Simon, 7 Gracie Square, New York, N.Y. 10028.
Alfred P. Slaner, 640 Fifth Ave., New York, N.Y. 10019.
Howard Sloan, 75 Maiden Lane, New York, N.Y.
George A. Smith, 17 Ames St. Rutherford, N.J. 07070.
Ruth P. Smith, 1 West 72nd St. New York, N.Y.
*Mrs. Randolph Smitherman, 617 Tinkerbell Rd., Chapel Hill, N.C. 27514.
*Mrs. M. R. Smitherman, 617 Tinkerbell Rd., Chapel, Hill, N.C. 27514.
George Soros, 25 Central Park South, New York, N.Y.
Leonard and Libbie Spacek, 1550 Lake Shore Drive, Chicago, Ill. 60610
L. M. Sperry, 20 Crest Road, Belvedere, Calif. 94920.
Mrs. Leonard M. Sperry, 9198 Cordell Dr., Los Angeles, Calif.
M/M Paul J. Sperry, 115 Central Park West, New York, N.Y. 10023.
V. Sperry, 500 Crestline Drive, Los Angeles, Calif. 90049.

---

* Mrs. Randolph Smitherman and Mrs. M. R. Smitherman may be same person.
* Dr. Vera Rubin may be same as Mrs. Vera Rubin listed at address above.

Mrs. Victoria H. Sperry, 500 Crestline Dr., Los Angeles, Calif. 90049.

Vicki Sperry, c/o Carol Moss, 335 S. Rimpau, Los Angeles, Calif.

Lyman Spitzer, 659 Lake Dr., Princeton, N.J. 08540.

Jon Splane, 619½ Third, Flint, Mich.

Fortney Stark, Jr., Security Bank Building, 1500 Newell Ave., Walnut Creek, Calif. 94596.

Dinah Starr, 198 Beacon St., Boston, Mass. 02116.

Leften Stavrianos, 53-109 Kam Hwy., Punaluu, Hawaii.

Hy Steirman, 1 Chesterfield Rd., Scarsdale, N.Y.

John A. Stephens, 4400 Via Abrigado, Hope Ranch, Calif.

Carl W. Stern, 55 Raycliff Terrace, San Francisco, Calif. 94115.

M/M Philip Stern, 2301 S Street, N.W., Washington, D.C. 20008.

Alvin Sternlieb, 20 Willowbrook Lane, Freeport, N.Y. 11520.

Dr. & Mrs. R. J. Stoller, 1100 Rivas Canyon, Pacific Palisades, Calif.

Martain and Elaine Stone, 10889 Wilshire Blvd., Los Angeles, Calif.

Mrs. Myron K. Stone, 56 East 80th St., New York, N.Y. 10021.

Robert C. Stover, 150 College Ave., Poughkeepsie, N.Y. 12603.

Donald B. Straus, 140 West 51st St., New York, N.Y. 10020.

Marvin A. Strin, 11110 Ohio Ave., West Los Angeles, Calif.

Bernard Stryer, 104 Raymond Ave., Millburn, N.J.

Lee J. Stull, New Delhi, Dept. of State, Washington, D.C.

John Sturges, 13063 Ventura Blvd., N. Hollywood, Calif. 91604.

Mark Swann, R.D. #1, New Park, Pa. 17352.

O. W. Switz, P.O. Box 723, Red Bank, N.J.

George H. Talbot, 125 East 4th St., Charlotte, N.C.; and 417 Hermitage Rd., Charlotte, N.C.

A. A. Taubman, Special Account, Southfield, Mich.

Michael Taylor, 32 Gramercy Park South, New York, N.Y.

Michael Tennenbaum, c/o Bear Sterns & Co., 1 Wall St., New York, N.Y.

Frank Thielen, Jr., P.O. Box 427, Baytown, Tex. 77520.

Lee B. Thomas, Sr., Box 1523, Louisville, Ky.

Matthew D. Thomases, 1450 Broadway, New York, N.Y.

J. B. Tietz, 410 Douglas Bldg., 257 S. Spring St., Los Angeles, Calif.

Bardyl Tirana, 3509 Lowell St., N.W., Washington, D.C. 20016.

John L. Tishman, 885 Park Avenue, New York, N.Y.

Belmont Towbin, C. E. Unterberg (No address).

Robert C. Townsend, 45 Sutton Place South, New York, N.Y.

R. C. Townsend, Duck Pond Road, Locust Valley, N.Y. 11560.

Mrs. Katharine W. Tremaine, 1512 Miramar Beach, Santa Barbara, Calif. 93108.

David H. Tucker, 10383 Barcan Circle, Columbia, Md. 20144.

Joyce B. Turner, 4948 S. Kimbark Ave., Chicago, Ill. 60615.

Eugene K. Twining, Commonwealth Building, Allentown, Pa.

Frances Vicario, North Bennington, Vt. 05257.

Fred Viehe, 9320 S.W. Eighth Ave., Portland, Ore. 97219.

Norman Wain, 15809 Onaway Rd., Shaker Heights, Ohio 44115.

Dr. George Wald, 21 Lakeview Ave., Cambridge, Mass.

Linda Wallace, 435 S. Lafayette, Los Angeles, Calif.

Ira Wallach, Central National Corp., 100 Park Ave., New York, N.Y.

Joan Warburg, 60 East 42nd St., New York, N.Y.

Maxine F. Warner, 100 Malibu Colony, Malibu, Calif.

Carmen Warschaw, 417 S. Hill St., #434, Los Angeles, Calif.

Samuel Warshauer, 187 Leroy St., Tenafly, N.J. 07670.

Jean S. Weaver, 445 El Arroyo, Hillsborough, Calif. 94010.

Robert Weil, 1880 Century Park East, Los Angeles, Calif. 90067.

Samuel Weiner, Jr., 451 West Broadway, New York, N.Y. 10012.

Howard Weingrow, 201 E .42nd St., New York, N.Y.

Howard A. Weiss, 209 South LaSalle St., Chicago, Ill.

Molly Weiss, 1040 North Lake Shore Drive, Chicago, Ill.

Robert G. Weiss, 209 South LaSalle St., Chicago, Ill.

Bernard Weissbourd, 111 East Wacker Dr., Chicago, Ill. 60601.

Stanley S. Weithorn, 405 Lexington Ave., New York, N.Y. 10017.

Mr. Wellington, Princeton, N.J.

Albert B. Wells, 250 Golden Hills Dr., Portola Valley, Calif.

Joseph P. Wells, 673 Second Ave., New York, N.Y. 10016.

Barbara Wheatland, P.O. Box 271, Topsfield, Mass. 01983.

Keith Wheelock, Todd Pond Rd., Lincoln, Mass.

Henry Willcox, 38 Dock Road, South Norwalk, Conn. 06854.
Harold Willens, 1122 Maple Ave., Los Angeles, Calif. 90015; and 321 South Bristol, Los Angeles, Calif.
Estelle Williams, 723 N. Elm Dr., Beverly Hills, Calif. 90210.
Charles E. Wilson, 4513 Coachman, Baytown, Tex.
Mrs. Catherine Winkler, 4660 Kenmore Ave., Alexandria, Va. 22304.
Werner F. Wolfen, Suite 900, Gateway East, Los Angeles, Calif.; or 1800 Ave. of the Stars, Los Angeles, Calif.
Louis Wolfson, Financier (No address).
Mrs. Dudley Wood, 320 E. 72nd St., New York, N.Y. 10021.
Miss Lucia Woods, 214 E. 70th, New York, N.Y. 10002.
Mrs. Elizabeth G. Woodward, 800 Seminole Ave., Philadelphia, Pa.
Frederick Worden, 45 Hilltop Road, Boston, Mass.
Lyn Wyman, 650 Nash, Menlo Park, Calif.
George Yntema, RFD 2, Box 80A, Manchester, Conn.
Quentin D. Young, M.D., 1418 E. 55th St., Chicago, Ill. 60615.
Floyd Yudelson, 9021 Melrose, Los Angeles, Calif.
Alejandro Zaffaroni, 214 Polhemus Ave., Atherton, Calif.
Meyer Zeiler, M.D., 710 North Walden Dr., Beverly Hills, Calif.

Abzug, Rep. Bella	MacLaine, Shirley
Armstrong, Robert	Mankiewicz, Frank
Brown, Willie L.	Martindell Anne
Caddell, Patrick	McPherson, Mike
Caplin, Mortimer	Meyers, Henry
Chayes, Dr. Abram	O'Brien, Lawrence
Clifford, Clark	Okun, Arthur M.
Cohen, Dick	Patterson, Basil
Cunningham, George	Pechman, Joseph A.
Daniels, Harley	Pokorny, Gene
Davis, Lon	Proxmire, Senator William
DeWind, Adrian	Rapp, Stan
Dougherty, Richard	Rubin, Miles
Duffey, Rev. Joe	Salinger, Pierre
Dutton, Frederick G.	Schultze, Charles L.
Farenthold, Frances (Sissy)	Scoville, Herbert Jr.
Gavin, Lt. Gen. James M. (Retired)	Smith, Floyd
Guggenheim, Charles	Stearnes, Rick
Halsted, Tom	Surrey, Stanley S.
Hart, Gary	Sylvester, Edward S., Jr.
Heller, Walter O.	Tobin, James
Himmelman, Harold	Van Dyck, Ted
Holum, John D.	Warnke, Paul C.
James, William S.	Weil, Gordon
Jones, Kirby	Westwood, Jean
Kimelman, Henry	Wexler, Anne
Kuh, Edwin	White, Cissy
LaRocque, Rear Adm. Gene (Retired)	Willens, Harold
Levett, Michael	York, Herbert F.
Lobell, Martin	

The Names

The following names from List #1 and List #2 are notable individuals who can easily be identified; they are listed by their occupation or profession at the time of the Nixon enemies lists. Others in both lists — especially List # 2 — are not so easily identified; readers may know some of the other names. Why some of these names appear on the Enemies Lists continues to be a mystery.

(What is also not known is which of these names incurred Nixon's personal wrath for one reason or another and which may have been added by Charles Colson, John Dean or others in Nixon's coterie.)

List # 1

I.W. Abel — organized labor leader.
Ralph Abernathy — civil rights leader.
Bella Abzug — member, U.S. House of Representatives.
Jack Anderson -- journalist/columnist.
Birch Bayh — U.S. Senator.
Leonard Bernstein — conductor/musician.
Jim Bishop — writer.
Derek Bok— president of Harvard University.
Kingman Brewster Jr. — U.S. diplomat.
McGeorge Bundy — U.S. diplomat.
Carol Channing— entertainer.
Marquis Childs -- writer/columnist.
Shirley Chisholm — first black woman elected to the House of
        Representatives; first black woman nominated for president
        (Democratic party).
Noam Chomsky — academic and activist.
Ramsey Clark — Attorney General in the Lyndon Johnson
        administration.
Clark Clifford — political advisor/Secretary of Defense in the Lyndon
        Johnson administration.

John Conyers — black member of the U.S. House of Representatives;
    served more than 50 years in the House.

Bill Cosby - entertainer.

Michael DeBakey — heart surgeon.

Ron Dellums — served 13 terms in the U.S. House of Representatives,
    prior to his House service, was Mayor of Oakland,
    Calif.

Robert Drinan — Jesuit priest, member of the U.S House of Rep-
    resentatives, activist.

Jane Fonda — actress.

J. William Fulbright — U.S. Senator.

J. Kenneth Galbraith — economist.

John Gardner — writer, professor.

Dick Gregory — activist.

Morton Halperin — government official, expert on foreign affairs
    civil rights, other areas.

Pete Hammil — writer.

Michael Harrington — early Democratic Socialist.

Walter Heller — economist.

Walter Hickel — Governor of Alaska, Secretary of the Interior in the
    Nixon administration.

Marvin Kalb — journalist. Served more than 30 years with CBS and
    NBC; has written a variety of books on politics and political
    philosophy.

Edward (Teddy) Kennedy -- Senator.

Morton Kondracke — journalist.

Joseph Kraft — journalist, speechwriter for John Kennedy.

John Lindsay — Mayor of New York.

Allard Lowenstein — politician, served one term in the U.S. House of
    Representatives.

Eugene McCarthy — U.S. Senator, challenged Lyndon Johnson during
    the Vietnam war.

George McGovern — politician. Lost to Nixon in a landslide in the
    1972 presidential election.

Mary McGrory — journalist, columnist, specialized in politics.

Robert McNamara — Secretary of Defense in the Kennedy and
    Johnson administrations.

Steve McQueen — actor.

Frank Mankiewicz — journalist, presidential advisor.

Ralph Metcalf — Olympic athlete, served four terms in the U.S. House of Representatives.

Walter Mondale — U.S. Senator, lost to Ronald Reagan in 1984 landslide.

Hans Morgenthau — foreign policy expert.

Stewart Mott — philanthropist, noted for liberal causes..

Ed Muskie — Senator, Secretary of State under Jimmy Carter.

Joe Namath — football star.

Gaylord Nelson — U.S. senator, established "Earth Day," specialist in environmental concerns.

Paul Newman — actor.

Wright Patman — member U.S. House of Representatives.

Gregory Peck — actor.

William Proxmire — U.S. Senator from Wisconsin.

Tony Randall — actor.

Charles Rangel — served in the U.S. House of Representatives 1971-2017.

James Reston — journalist.

Richard Rovere — political journalist.

Carl Rowan — journalist, Assistant Secretary of State in the Kennedy administration, Ambassador to Finland.

Baynard Rustin — civil rights and gay rights activist.

Paul Samuelson — leading economist.

Arthur Schlesinger Jr. — historian, social critic.

Sargent Shriver — part of the Kennedy family, diplomat, politician, activist. Key figure in creating the Peace Corps, Job Corps, other facets of the 1960s War on Poverty.

Ted Sorenson — speechwriter, close advisor to John Kennedy.

Louis Stokes— served 15 terms in the U.S. House of Representatives from the Cleveland area.

Robert Straus — veteran Democratic politics and policy expert; his career dated from Lyndon Johnson's first congressional campaign in 1937.

Barbra Streisand — singer.

Jack Valenti — special assistant to Lyndon Johnson.

Sandor Vanocur — major political reporter of the 1960s and 1970s.

George Wallace — four-term Governor of Alabama,; opposed the Civil
    Rights programs, opposed desegregation. Ran against Lyndon
    Johnson in the 1964 Democratic primaries.
Paul Warnke — led a variety of top administrative positions,
    including General Counsel to the Secretary of
    Defense in the Lyndon Johnson administration.
Tom Wicker — journalist.

List # 2

This list, although it is longer than List #1, appears to contain almost
no known political/governmental figures; which means it was clearly
compiled by others apart from List 1 and perhaps for different
reasons.   It contains   only a very few   cultural or entertainment
names:

Herb Alpert — musician —co-owner A & M records (then, later sold).
Polly Bergen — actress.
Alexander Calder — internationally-known artist.
Oscar Dystel — paperback book publisher, Bantam Books, New York.
Max Factor — beauty products executive.
Malcolm Forbes, publisher **Forbes** magazine.
John Kenneth Galbraith —   economist, diplomat.
Ralph Gleason — musician, one of the founders of **Rolling Stone**
    magazine.
Gene Hackman — actor.
Hugh Hefner — founder, publisher, **Playboy** magazine.
Burt Lancaster — actor.
Frank Lautenberg — U.S. Senator, New Jersey.
Norman Lear — producer ("All in the Family").
Howard Metzenbaum — U.S. Senator, Ohio.
Stewart Mott — philanthropist.
Paul Newman — actor.
Joanne Newman — actress.
Georgia O'Keefe — artist.
George Soros — philanthropist.
Louis Wolfson - -financier.

List #2 has a supplemental list, including:

Bella Abzug — on List 1.
Willie Brown — former San Francisco Mayor.
Clark Clifford — U.S. Secretary of Defense.
Frances "Sissy" Farenthold — Texas politician and human rights
    activist.
Lt. Gen. James Gavin — U.S. Army
Rear Admiral Gene LaRocque — U.S. Navy
Shirley MacLaine — actress.
Frank Mankiewicz — Journalist.
Lawrence O'Brien — Democratic Party official.
William Proxmire — U.S. Senator, Wisconsin.
Pierre Salinger — journalist and politician.
Paul Warnke — also on List #1.
Anne Wexler — activist.

4   The Enemies List denouement

When the Internal Revenue Service issued its December, 1973 report it was game over for the Nixon administration's Enemies List project.

The Enemies List became public, and more importantly, the I.R.S. showed itself unwilling to aid and abet the Nixon people in their persecution of their enemies.

And what else? Did any of the Nixon people face arrest for attempting to coerce the I.R.S. into conspiring with the Nixon people? Apparently there were no arrests in this regard.

Did any of the Nixon people face condemnation from Congress for their acts? None.

Did any of them lose their jobs in the Nixon White House? Surely not — they were all good foot soldiers for Nixon.

Did their remarkable hubris cost anything at all?

Not immediately — not then — their hubris went unchecked until the I.R.S. said "no, we won't do this."

But it can be said that the Enemies List project directly led to the Nixon administration's establishment of the "Plumbers" inside the Nixon White House — the Plumbers to "stop leaks" — then the attempted break-in of Daniel Ellsberg's psychiatrist's office in the Pentagon Papers case and the break-in of the Democratic party offices in the Watergate complex in Washington, D.C.

In fact, unknown at the time, the Enemies List project was the first wave ... in a slow-growing but eventually relentless tsunami of scandal that would engulf and destroy the Nixon presidency.

5   Watergate

It has been both the most significant political scandal of the twentieth century and the premier reporting/journalism story of those times.

Watergate is now the generic name of any political scandal; any scandal du jour is now followed by the suffix-gate. This-gate and that-gate, (i.e., Bridgegate — the 2013 New Jersey political scandal under Gov. Chris Christie, which seriously damaged his 2016 presidential run) and others now largely forgotten.

Broadcasters and pundits have since used the phrase "This XXX-gate is bigger than Watergate." None have been.

Perhaps emboldened by their own hubris in the Enemies List operation — the Nixon people went further.

On January 27, 1972, G. Gordon Liddy, Finance Counsel for the Nixon Committee for the Re-Election of the president (which had the oddly unsettling but ultimately appropriate acronym CREEP) met with CRP's acting Chairman Jeb Stuart Magruder, Attorney General John Mitchell and Presidential counsel John Dean. The subject: covert activities against the Democratic Party. These activities were surely unethical and just as surely illegal. The first plan wasn't scuttled because it was unethical or illegal, just unworkable. They met again two months later and the second plan was accepted.

John Mitchell approved the second version of the plan: to break into the Democratic headquarters in the Watergate complex and photograph certain documents and install listening devices (bugs) in office telephones to overhear Democratic party conversations.

Involved were two former C.I.A. officers, E. Howard Hunt and James McCord. McCord was Security Coordinator after John Mitchell resigned as Attorney General to serve as CREEP chairman.

The crew booked room 419 at the Howard Johnson motel, across from the Watergate complex so they could observe activities in the Democratic headquarters.

'After midnight on Saturday 17, 1972, Watergate security guard Frank Wills discovered one door has been sabotaged with duct tape—the tape allowed the parking garage door to be closed but not locked. He removed the tape, assuming there was nothing to that — just a prank perhaps. He subsequently returned and found duct tape on the door again. This time he called the police.

A lookout, Alfred Baldwin, in the Howard Johnson motel room ascots the street failed to see a police car on street in front of the Watergate complex; nor did he see police searching the Democratic headquarters. By the time he did see activity it was too late.

Police arrested five men: Virgilio Gonzalez, Barnard Barker, James McCord, Eugenio Martinez and Frank Sturgis.

The Washington Post reported that the police found "lockpicks and door jimmies, almost $2,300 in cash, most of it in $100 bills with the serial numbers in sequence ... a short wave receiver that could pick up police calls, 40 rolls of unexposed film, two 35 mm cameras and three pen-sized tear gas guns."

The five were charged with attempted burglary and attempted interception of telephone and other communications.

Later, John Dean wrote:

> The report of the arrest in the early morning hours of June 17, 1972 of five men who had broken into the Watergate complex offices of the Democratic National committee (DNC), wearing business suits and surgical gloves, their pockets stuffed with hundred dollar bills, was something like a scene from a circa 1940s low-budget black-and-white gangster B movie. This caught-in-the-act stupidity seemed too dumb to be ours, since the undertaking was so completely illegal and inexplicably risky, not to mention obviously bungled. But this political surveillance debacle *did* turn out to be ours, the work of a ham-fisted team of amateurs assembled by G. Gordon Liddy, a former Nixon White House staff member who was then serving as general counsel for the finance operation of the Committee to Re-elect the President.... This was, in fact, the opening scene of the worst political scandal of the twentieth century and the beginning of the end of the Nixon presidency.

The break-in was initially judged to be nothing more than a third-rate burglary.

Except for the evidence — $2,300 in cash in $100 bills, in sequence, the short wave receiver, the film, the cameras and the tear-gas guns.

And the interview statements: when the police interviewed one of the C.I.A. officers : this was the exchange:

"What is your status?"

"Retired."

"Retired from what?"

"The C. I. A."

Why would a retired C.I.A. officer be involved in a third-rate burglary?

And the others — except for James McCord —they were all called "Cuban freedom fighters." Why?

When this scandal began, neither Carl Bernstein nor Bob Woodward had much experience on *The Washington Post*. (The term "cub reporter" has not been used much since Ernest Hemingway began his writing career with a seven-month stint as a reporter on *The Kansas City Star*. October 1, 1917 to April 30,1918.)

Woodward has worked at *The Washington Post* for only nine months; Bernstein had dropped out of college, began working at *The Washington Star* when he was 16 and had been a full-time reporter for *The Post* since 1966 — only about six years.

They got the story because it appeared to be *only* a third-rate burglary, which deserved little news space in the paper.

The 5 W's and the W in basic journalism —

They learned about the cash, the short wave receiver — the cameras, film

Why?

Why all this for a third-rate burglary?

And. the C.I.A. connection.

Why?

Why were retired C.I.A. employees involved in this?

Who else was involved?

Where did this story lead?

To pin down the facts, they resolved to verify every fact from two sources — from two interview subjects — they could sometimes get facts from one source, but seldom matching facts from two.

The Watergate mystery unraveled glacially slowly.

A timeline shows how slowly:

- June 12, 1972. Five men arrested while trying to bug the Democratic National committee's headquarters at the Watergate, a hotel and office building in Washington, D.C. A day later, White House press secretary Ron Ziegler famously called the Watergate break-in a "third-rate burglary." At a press conference June 22, President Nixon denied that the White House was involved in the incident.

- June 19,1972, the press reported that one of the burglars was a Republican Party security aide.

- August 1, 1972. *The Washington Post* reported that a $25,000 check intended for Nixon's 1972 reelection campaign was deposited in the bank account of one of the Watergate burglars. It was one of the first developments linking the DNC break-in to Nixon's campaign.

- August 29, 1972. At a news conference Nixon stated that (John) Dean had conducted a through investigation of the incident; in fact, Dean had done nothing of the kind. Nixon also said "I can say categorically that — no one in the White House staff, no one in the Administration, presently employed, was involved in this very bizarre incident."

- Oct., 10, 1972. *The Post* reports the FBI hah concluded the Watergate break-in was part of a broader spying effort connected to Nixon's campaign. News of the FBI's findings came two weeks later after

The Post reported that former Attorney General John Mitchell, who stepped down earlier that year, had controlled a secret fund that paid for spying on the Democratic Party.

- Jan. 6, 1973. The trial for the Watergate break-in begins. G. Gordon Liddy, a former Nixon aide, and James McCord, a one-time Nixon aide and former CIA operative, are convicted for their roles in spearheading the Watergate break-in.

- April 30,1973. The scandal reaches the White House, as senior White House aides H.R. Haldeman and John Ehrlichman resign over Watergate. Attorney General Richard Kleindienst also resigns, and John Dean, the White House counsel, gets fired.

- May 18,1973. Attorney General Eliot Richardson appoints Archibald Cox as special prosecutor to lead the investigation into Nixon's reelection campaign and Watergate. Cox was a respected attorney and law professor, and had served as the United States Solicitor General under Presidents John F. Kennedy and Lyndon Johnson. Cox's appointment comes one day after the Senate Watergate Committee begins its public hearings on the scandal. The committee's hearings are nationally televised and, along with Cox's investigation, marks a new phase in the Watergate scandal. It is at these Senate hearings that then-Senator Howard Baker (R. Term.) asks one of the most famous questions in American politics: "What did the president know and when did he know it?"

- July 23, 1973. Nixon, who taped his conversations and calls in (his Oval) office, refuses to give Cox and Senate Watergate investigators the recordings, which became known the "Nixon tapes." The tapes were believed to contain critical evidence of a cover-up of Nixon's involvement in the break-in; the previous month, John Dean, former White House counsel, acknowledged that he had talked with Nixon about the Watergate matter dozens of times. After Nixon refused to turn the tapes over, both Cox and Senate investigators issue subpoenas for the material.

- Oct. 20, 1973. The day that became known as the "Saturday Night Massacre." Attorney General Richardson and Deputy Attorney General William Ruckelshaus both resign the same night after refusing Nixon's order to fire Cox. Robert Bork, the solicitor general who was acting as attorney general, then followed Nixon's order and fired Cox. (Later Bork became a candidate for a position on the Supreme Court; because of his actions in the Saturday Night Massacre — and other events — he lost the possible position on the Supreme Court. Critics of Bork said it was only poetic justice.) Nixon's push to oust Cox, who was leading the independent investigation into White House misconduct, sparked intense criticism across the political spectrum. Four weeks later, on Nov. 17, Nixon issued his memorable denial: "I am not a crook."

- May 4,1974. The House Judiciary Committee starts impeachment proceedings against Nixon.

- July 24, 1974. In an unanimous ruling, the Supreme Court orders Nixon to release the tape recordings. The decision came two months after the White House gave the House Judiciary Committee edited transcripts of Nixon's conversations, but did not not turn over the actual tapes. (One of the tapes, called the "Smoking Gun" tape confirmed Nixon's deep and complete involvement in the Watergate cover-up. When that tape was revealed to Congress and to the public, support for Nixon evaporated in Congress.)

- July 27-30, 1974. The House Judiciary Committee passes three articles of impeachment against Nixon, for obstruction of justice, misuse of power and contempt of Congress. By approving the charges, the committee sent the impeachment to the floor for a full House vote, but it never occurred.

- Aug. 8, 1974. Nixon resigns. In his resignation speech, Nixon said. "I have never been a quitter. To leave office before my term is completed is abhorrent to every instinct in my body. But as president, I must put the interest of America first."

He will be forever known as the first and perhaps the only president to resign while in office. He spent the rest of his days working to rehabilitate his image and reputation.

Richard Nixon died in New York April 22,1994, at 81.

The Press

The connection between the break-in and the re-election committee was highlighted by media coverage—in particular investigative coverage by *The Washington Post* and *The New York Times*. (Despite some initial skepticism by editors among the staff of *The Post*.) The coverage dramatically increased publicity and consequent political and legal repercussions. Relying heavily upon anonymous sources, *Post* reporters Woodward and Bernstein uncovered information suggesting that knowledge of the break-in, and attempts to cover it up, led deeply into the upper reaches of the Justice Department, FBI, CIA and the White House. Woodward and Bernstein interviewed Judy Hoback Miller, the bookkeeper for Nixon, who revealed to them information about the mishandling of funds and records being destroyed.

During this early period, most of the media faced to grasp the full implications of the scandal (even Woodward and Bernstein didn't know where this story was going); many publications focused on other aspects of the 1972 Nixon presidential election. Many outlets ignored or played down Woodward and Bernstein's scoops. *The Washington Star-News* and *The Los Angeles Times* ran articles that erroneously discredited articles by Woodward and Bernstein. After *The Washington Post* ran articles revealing that H. R. Haldeman made payments to the Watergate burglars from a secret fund, *The Chicago Tribune* and *The Philadelphia Inquirer* failed to publish the articles, but did publish White House denials the next day. The White House also sought to isolate coverage by *The Post* by unceasingly attacking that newspaper, while declining to criticize other damaging articles about the scandal from *The New York Times* and *Time* magazine.

After it was learned that some of the convicted burglars wrote to Judge John Sirica alleging a high-level cover-up, the media shifted its focus. *Time Magazine* described Nixon as undergoing "dally hell and very little trust." The distrust between the press and the Nixon administration was mutual and greater then usual due to lingering dissatisfaction with events from the Vietnam war. (Most presidents harbor mixed sentiments about the press, covering their administrations). At the same time, public distrust of the media was polled at more than 40 percent.

Nixon and top administration officials often discussed using government agencies to "get" (or retaliate against) those they perceived as hostile media operations. Such activities had happened before Watergate. At the request of Nixon's White House in 1969, The FBI tapped the phones of five reporters. In 1971, the White House requested an audit of the tax returns of the editor of *Newsday*, after wrote a series of articles about the financial dealings of Charles "Bebe" Rebozo, a close friend of Richard Nixon.

The administration and its supporters accused the media of making "wild accusations," putting too much emphasis on the Watergate break-in and cover-up scandal and having a liberal bias against the Nixon administration. Nixon said, in a May 1974 interview with supporter Baruch Korff, that if he had followed the liberal policies that he thought the media preferred, "Watergate would have been a blip." The media noted that most of the reporting turned out to be accurate; the competitive nature of the media guaranteed wide-spread coverage of the growing and growing scandal.

Bob Woodard and Carl Bernstein eventually earned Pulitzer Prizes for their coverage of Watergate. Enrollment in journalism schools reached an all-time high; incoming college and university journalism students across the country all wanted to be the next Woodwards and Bernsteins.

One of the most fascinating aspects of the Woodward and Bernstein coverage was the anonymous source "Deep Throat," named after an infamous pornographic film released about the same time.

Deep Throat was a friend of Woodward's that Woodward had cultivated long before Watergate. Woodward and Deep Throat occasionally met in a deserted parking garage late at night during the period of June 1972 to January 1973, when Woodward needed help understanding how the story was progressing. They had first talked by telephone, but Deep Throat feared — and Woodward also feared — their phones could be tapped; thus the meetings in the deserted parking garage. (Deep Throat was played dramatically in the film version of *All the President's Men* by Hal Holbrook.)

Early in the interplay between the anonymous source and Bob Woodward, the source was termed "My Friend," at *The Washington Post*, but Woodward and others realized that the initials **M.F.** could easily be deciphered as **M**ark **F**elt, the second in command at the FBI. *Post* editor Howard Simons began using Deep Throat, as the garage meetings with Woodward were on "deep background": no source name could be used.

(It was said that the film "Deep Throat," released in 1972, brought pornographic films into the mainstream of American culture.)

The source Deep Throat told Woodward of Howard Hunt's involvement in the Watergate break-in and that the White House considered the stakes very high. Deep Throat warned Woodward that the FBI wanted to know where *The Post* and other papers were getting their information; as they were uncovering a wider web of crimes than the FBI had disclosed.

Bob Woodward faithfully kept the secret of the identity of Deep Throat a secret for over 30 years. In *All the President's Men*, Deep Throat was described as "a source in the Executive Branch who had access to information at CEP (the Committee to Re-elect the President) as well as the White House."

Vanity Fair magazine finally revealed the secret in its July 2005 issue — Deep Throat *had* been Mark Felt, the number two man in the FBI. Released from his decades-long obligation keep the secret any longer, Woodward published a book *The Secret Man: The Story of Watergate's Deep Throat*, later in 2005.

Mark Felt died Dec. 18, 2008, at 95.

6 Watergate Convictions

How many people in the Nixon administration were charged with crimes relating to Watergate?

> 69 were charged with crimes.
> 48 were found guilty.

Quite simply, it is staggering how many top Nixon officials served time in prison for their roles in the Watergate affair. These are some of the key figures during that time:

- John Mitchell, Attorney General of the United States, who resigned to become Director of the Committee to Re-elect the President, convicted of perjury about his involvement in the Watergate break-in. Served 19 months of a one-to-four-year sentence.

- Richard Kleindienst, Attorney General, convicted of "refusing to answer questions" (contempt of court); given one month in jail.

- Jeb Stuart Magruder, Deputy Director of the Committee to Re-elect the President, pled guilty to one count of conspiracy to the burglary, and was sentenced to 10 months to four years in prison, of which he served 7 months before being paroled.

- Frederick C. LaRue, advisor to John Mitchell, convicted of obstruction of justice. He served four and one half months.

- H.R Haldeman, Chief of Staff for Nixon, convicted of conspiracy to the burglary, obstruction of justice, and perjury Served 18 months in prison.

- John Erlichman, Counsel to Nixon, convicted of conspiracy to the burglary, obstruction of justice and perjury. Served 18 months in prison.

- John W. Dean, Counsel to Nixon, convicted of obstruction justice, later reduced to felony offenses and sentenced to time already served, which totaled four months.

- Egil Krogh, aide to John Ehrlichman, sentenced to six months for his part in the Daniel Ellsberg case.

- Dwight L. Chapin, deputy assistant to Nixon, convicted of perjury.

- Maurice Stans, United States Secretary of Commerce, who resigned to become Finance Chairman of the Committee to Re-elect the President, convicted of multiple counts of illegal campaigning, fined $5,000 (in 1975, equivalent to over $23,300 today.)

- Herbert Kalmbach, personal attorney to Nixon, convicted of illegal campaigning. Served 191 days in prison and fined $10,000 (in 1974, equivalent to over $50,800 today).

- Charles W. Colson, special counsel to Nixon, convicted to obstruction of justice. Served 7 months in federal prison.

- Herbert L. Porter, aide to the Committee to Re-elect the President. Convicted of perjury.

- G. Gordon Liddy, Special Investigations Group, convicted of masterminding the burglary, original sentence of up to 20 years in prison. Served four and one-half years in federal prison.

- E. Howard Hunt, security consultant, convicted of masterminding and overseeing the burglary. Original sentence of up to 35 years in prison. Served 33 months in prison.

- James W. McCord. Jr., convicted of six charges of burglary, conspiracy and wiretapping. Served two months in prison.

- Virgilio Gonzales, convicted of burglary, original sentence of up to 40 years in prison. Served 13 months in prison.

- Bernard Barker, convicted of burglary, original sentence of up to 40 years in prison. Served 18 months in prison.

- Eugenio Martinez, convicted of burglary, original sentence of up to 40 years in prison. Served 15 months in prison.

- Frank Sturgis, convicted of burglary, original sentence of up to 40 years in prison. Served 10 months in prison.

7   Watergate denouement

Why did the Enemies List happen?

Why did the Watergate scandal happen?

Put another way, why did Nixon allow the Enemies List project to go forward? To eventually include over 700 names ....

Why did he cover-up the Watergate affair, which cost him his presidency?

Nixon resigned in 1974; three years later he agreed to a series of interviews with British broadcaster David Frost; Frost's production company agreed to pay Nixon for the interviews. Segments were shown on American television but American media companies were reluctant to broadcast them because U.S. media companies don't believe in "checkbook journalism," i.e., paying sources for information or interviews, but the Frost interviews were too important to ignore.

The first broadcast reached 45 million viewers, a record for a political interview then and a record which still stands today.

The 12 interview sessions began on March 23, 1977, with three interviews per week over four weeks. They were taped in California for more than two hours a day, on Mondays, Wednesday and Fridays, for a total of 28 hours and 45 minutes.

What were Nixon's core beliefs? What was his moral center? What guided him? What allowed him to approve the Enemies List and essentially approve — and cover-up the Watergate affair?

At his core — the keyword is *amoral.*

Essentially, Nixon had no core beliefs to guide him. No north star of moral certainty. No inner resolve of strength.

During the third episode, broadcast May 19, 1977, Nixon revealed his inner being in one stunning sentence:

Well, when the president does it.
that means it is not illegal.

Annotated Bibliography

Bernstein, Carl and Bob Woodward. *All the President's Men.* New York: Simon and Schuster, 1974.

Widely considered the greatest reporting/journalism story of the twentieth century; how two young reporters from *The Washington Post*, doggedly and eventually broke the Watergate story. In print in various editions since 1974.

Dean, John W. *Blind Ambition: The White House Years.* New York: Simon and Schuster, 1976.

Dean's memoirs, published after Watergate.

_____. *The Nixon Defense: What He Knew and When He Knew It.* New York: Penguin Books, 2014.

Massively detailed (746 pp.) analysis of Nixon and Watergate.

Weiner, Tim. *One Man Against the World: The Tragedy of Richard Nixon.* New York: Henry Holt, 2015.

Perhaps the most negative of the Nixon books, hypnotic and intensive.

Woodward, Bob. *The Secret Man: The Story of Watergate's Deep Throat.* New York: Simon and Schuster, 2005.

Note: the website www.paperlessarchives.com has the same files as in this book, but that website material has no commentary, analysis, conclusions, bibliography or any other material; it is simply the raw files of the Enemies List data.

Appendix: Nixon's Grand Jury Testimony

President Nixon was compelled to give testimony to a Grand Jury June 26, 1975; one of the very few times a sitting president has been called before a Grand Jury.

After a series of questions by attorney Jay Horowitz, about whether the White House attempted to influence the Internal Revenue service or to audit or otherwise harass Lawrence O'Brien, a leading Democratic Party strategy leader, Nixon makes a break: in the questioning and makes a statement to defend his political tactics, to assert that as a candidate he was the victim of abuses of power in which the IRS and the FBI were used against him, and that the current investigation was one-sided, ignoring the tactics of his opponents:

> But I think that it is time, and perhaps the Special Prosecutor, when he files his final report, will have one paragraph in for history; it is time for us to recognize that in politics in America, and this is not excusable, but it does explain it to an extent, particularly where the highest office in the land is involved, and even in some circumstances where campaigns for governor in major states or senators are involved, that in politics some pretty rough tactics are used.

This was not an apology from Nixon, rather just a rationale for behavior. (This appears on transcript page 216, page number shown at top right corner.)

1

P R O C E E D I N G S

MR. RUTH: Let me go on the record.

This is a reminder that this is a continuation of yesterday's sworn deposition, that therefore the oath continues today and, in addition, you may continue, of course, as you did yesterday, to consult with your attorneys who are here, Mr. Miller and Mr. Mortenson, consult with them at any time you wish.

The attorneys here today, in addition to Mr. Davis and myself, are Mr. Hecht, at the far end of the table, and Mr. Horowitz nwxt to him.

Whereupon,

RICHARD M. NIXON,

having been previously duly sworn, was examined and testified further as follows:

E X A M I N A T I O N

BY MR. HOROWITZ:

Q   Sir, my name is Jay Horowitz and Mr. Hecht is next to me, to my right.

We intend to ask you some questions relevant to the Grand Jury's investigation, which is, specifically, into allegations that White House affiliated persons attempted to influence the IRS to audit or otherwise harass Mr. Lawrence F. O'Brien, Sr., and questions which are also relevant to the Grand Jury's investigation that the White

HOOVER REPORTING CO., INC.
320 Massachusetts Avenue, N.E.
Washington, D.C. 20002
(202) 546-6666

2

171

House affiliated persons attempted to secure from the Internal

Revenue Service documents --

    A.   Could I interrupt, please?

        In other words, the Special Prosecutor's Office

is only interested in the IRS harassment activities insofar

as it deals with Mr. O'Brien? It is not interested in any

harassment that the IRS may have done or is doing or has

done with regard to, say, me, my friends, or anything like

that? Am I clear that your sole interest is IRS activity

with regard to O'Brien?

    Q.   Not exactly. In this particular investigation,

this particular Grand Jury investigation --

    A.   Do you have other Grand Jury investigations in

which you are applying a single standard, in which you are

looking, seeing whether the IRS has harassed other people?

    Q.   Well, Mr. Nixon, this particular investigation is

directed to these allegations.

    A.   I think you have answered my question.

        Go ahead.

        MR. RUTH: Could I just interrupt, sir?

        THE WITNESS: Sure, anytime.

        MR. RUTH: As you know, sir, we are limited by a

charter that we operate under that limits our jurisdiction

to certain factual situations having to do with White House

staff members, presidential appointees and the 1972

HOOVER REPORTING CO., INC.
320 Massachusetts Avenue, N.E.
Washington, D.C. 20002
(202) 546-6666

74

3

172

1 presidential campaign and other matters. We can only investi-

2 gate that which is within our charter.

3 THE WITNESS: Your charter, however, Mr. Ruth, as

4 I understand it, is not limited simply to one political

5 party. It covers both, does it not?

6 MR. RUTH: That is correct.

7 THE WITNESS: In other words, harassment, if it

8 happened in the other political party, would also be part of

9 your charter, would it not?

10 MR. RUTH: Only if it were by presidential

11 appointees from January 20, 1969. The Department of Justice

12 has to do the rest. We are quite limited in what we are able

13 to do.

14 THE WITNESS: Yes. I just wanted to know, and

15 you have quite enough on your plate without having more to do.

16 Sorry, Mr. Horowitz. Go ahead. I know you have a

17 lot of questions.

18 BY MR. HOROWITZ:

19 Q I think I indicated, sir, that one thrust of this

20 Grand Jury investigation relates to efforts to get the IRS

21 to audit or otherwise harass Mr. O'Brien.

22 The other leg of it, if you will, relates to

23 attempts to secure documents from the Internal Revenue

24 Service, attempts allegedly made by White House affiliated

25 persons for the purpose of disseminating such documents or

HOOVER REPORTING CO., INC.
320 Massachusetts Avenue, N.E.
Washington, D.C. 20002
(202) 546-6666

4

1   distributing them to unauthorized persons, that is, persons

2   who would not in the ordinary or legal course have access to

3   such internal revenue Service information.

4   Now, those are the two legs of this particular

5   and very specifically, as you pointed out, specifically

6   limited investigation.

7   I will focus most of my questions upon various

8   documents which we have, to a certain extent, been provided

9   by your counsel in the past, and we have provided them prior

10 to our meeting here today, and most of the questions will be

11 by myself, although near the end probably Mr. Hecht will put

12 some questions to you as well.

13   Now, one further thing by way of prefatory remarks

14 and background, and hopefully we can assist in refreshing

15 your recollection.

16   Where we are focused, sir, is on the summer, and

17 primarily July, August and September of 1972, and during that

18 period there was an extensive Internal Revenue Service

19 investigation of Howard Hughes, whether personally or his

20 affiliated company, but that conglomerate of interests, and

21 it was in the course of that investigation that the Internal

22 Revenue Service developed information which established that

23 Mr. O'Brien and two associates of his, one by the name of

24 Joseph Napolitan, N-a-p-o-l-i-t-a-n, and one by the name of

25 Claud de Sautels -- I am not sure of the spelling of that one.

HOOVER REPORTING CO., INC.
320 Massachusetts Avenue, N.E.
Washington, D.C. 20002
(202) 546-6666

5   174

1   A.   I think it is not Mr. Napolitan, it is Napolitan

2   Associates. It is a public relations firm.

3   Q.   (Continuing) -- that those individuals had

4   received various funds from Mr. Hughes back in 1969 and 1970.

5   Now we are going to focus specifically, starting

6   on a meeting that you had with Messrs. Haldeman and Ehrlich-

7   man on August 3 of 1972. But before I do that, since this

8   information developed prior to that time in the course of the

9   investigation, could you tell us when you first became aware

10   of the fact that information indicating that O'Brien and his

11   associates had received funds from Hughes or Hughes affili-

12   ated companies had come to surface through the IRS investi-

13   gation?

14   A.   Well, we are talking about two different problems

15   here, and I want to be quite precise.

16   First, is the problem in which you have jurisdic-

17   tion, and that is the alleged harassment of Mr. O'Brien by

18   the IRS; and, second, when I became aware of the fact that

19   the Hughes Company had Mr. O'Brien on retainer. Is that your

20   question?

21   Q.   Well, no, I made it a little unclear, I think.

22   What I am interested in is when you first became aware that

23   the Internal Revenue Service had developed information that

24   the Hughes Company had O'Brien on retainer.

25   A.   My first recollection of having knowledge that the

175

6

1 Internal Revenue Service had information with regard to the

2 retainer by Mr. O'Brien was sometime in the summer of 1972.

3 However, I should point out that I had been

4 informed long ago, and I think this was public knowledge,

5 that O'Brien was, O'Brien and Senator Hubert Humphrey's son-

6 in-law and others, were on retainer with the Hughes organiza-

7 tion. I learned that as early as, oh, 1969 or 1970. Whether

8 the IRS knew it then or was interested in it then, I do

9 not know.

10 Q. You say in the summer of 1972. Can you tell us

11 who first informed you that the Internal Revenue Service was

12 inquiring into that matter?

13 A. No, I can't remember who specifically informed me

14 that the Internal Revenue Service was looking into that

15 matter.

16 Q. When you first heard that they were looking into

17 that matter, what did you understand they were looking into?

18 A. What I understood they were looking into was the

19 fact that Mr. Hughes and the various other people that the

20 recorder has already put into her notes were receiving very,

21 very substantial retainers from Mr. Hughes or from, I should

22 say, the Hughes organization, and the question was whether

23 those retainers were for services rendered or whether those

24 retainers might be used for the purpose of being funneled

25 into political campaigns. That is, in sum, a number of

176

of conversations, you see.

    Q   All right, I think it will assist, and perhaps it was about the time of these first notes to refer then to notes of August 3, 1972, which we have been provided by your counsel sometime ago, and they refer to a meeting between yourself, Mr. Haldeman and Mr. Ehrlichman in the morning, and I will mark that D-1, which serves as a Grand Jury designation.

    A   Uh-huh.

                  (The document referred to was marked Exhibit D-1 for identification.)

    THE WITNESS: Where did it take place?

    MR. HOROWITZ: That I cannot tell you.

    THE WITNESS: Sorry.

    BY MR. HOROWITZ:

    Q   Now, these notes, like others --

    A   I would have thought my counsel would have furnished you with tapes where it took place.

    MR. HOROWITZ: We now understand it took place in Washington, D. C.

    THE WITNESS: All right, go ahead.

    I was just curious whether it was San Clemente. It may help to refresh my recollection.

177

8

BY MR. HOROWITZ:

Q.   These notes, like other notes we will get into, are fragmentary in part, and what I propose to do with these notes, which I will do with later notes, is to read those notations on the notes to you which directly appear to pertain to our investigation.

A.   You, of course, will have a copy for me so I can read along with you?

Q.   Let me give you D-1.

A.   I can see why teachers hate to grade papers. They are so hard to read, the writing, let alone to know what they meant by it.

Go ahead.

Q.   Under (1), which is headed IRS and Justice, there is a note, "Investigations of us when we were out," a note pertaining to Ed Nixon-Oceanographic Fund, and in the following notes, "Use our power, contributors, Larry O'Brien."

Can you tell us what that conversation was as to that portion, "Use our powers, contributors, Larry O'Brien"?

A.   Perhaps it would be best for me to, rather than to take that out of context, to put it in context, which I know you would want, so that you have a total story.

When I referred to investigations of us when we were out, I was referring to the fact that the IRS notoriously had a well-deserved reputation for being used politically,

178

9

1 and in some instances developing within its own bureaucracy

2 a partisan political viewpoint.

3   For example, when I ran for Vice President in

4 1952, the IRS, I understand, and I am not sure from whom they

5 got the orders, but from very high sources, took my income

6 tax returns and made them available to a Washington columnist,

7 Mr. Drew Pearson, and to the Saint Louis Post Dispatch.

8   Those returns were used in the campaign against me.

9 They were not -- obviously, whoever got the returns only put

10 out those portions of the returns that might be derogatory.

11 The next year I gave the whole return out, all of my returns,

12 to Look Magazine, and they were printed, and that is when

13 Look was still being published.

14   In 1962, the IRS again -- I was then, of course,

15 out of power -- I was not in Washington -- I was running for

16 Governor -- the IRS instituted an intensive investigation

17 which was a dry hole for them.

18   As a matter of fact, at the end I think they owed

19 us some money. But an intensive investigation with regard

20 to the purchase of my house, in Truesdale Estates, they

21 leaked that information to the press, in this instance to the

22 California press, to the Los Angeles Times and the Long

23 Beach paper, and I have a letter, ironically, which I

24 received from the man who was the head of the field office

25 of the IRS, which I would like to submit for --

HOOVER REPORTING CO., INC.
320 Massachusetts Avenue, N.E.
Washington, D.C. 20002
(202) 546-6666

179

10   1   THE WITNESS: Can I submit something, a document

2   in evidence?

3   MR. RUTH: Yes, sir.

4   THE WITNESS: (Continuing) -- which I will submit

5   as D-3.

6   MR. HECHT: 2 - sir.

7   THE WITNESS: D-2.

8   (The document referred to

9   was marked Exhibit D-2

10   for identification.)

11   THE WITNESS: This is the letter of November 13,

12 1973. It is to Miss Woods, my secretary. I will leave out

13 the --

14   MR. RUTH: Excuse me, sir, does this pertain to

15 any particular --

16   THE WITNESS: The IRS, it certainly does.

17   MR. RUTH: Does it have to do with a tax situation

18 of yours?

19   THE WITNESS: You listen and you will see.

20   MR. RUTH: Could I just explain a problem we have?

21   THE WITNESS: Sure.

22   MR. RUTH: We have an outstanding indictment

23 having to do with a tax situation with Mr. De Marco and Mr.

24 Newman, and we are not allowed to use the Grand Jury to get

25 into that, and I just wanted to make sure --

180

THE WITNESS: No, this is November 13, 1973. It has to do with the IRS harassment of an individual who had been Vice President, who is running for Governor of California, about his returns, and I am sure the IRS and this group have no interest in that sort of thing. I mean obviously if you did, you would lose your jobs.

It says, "I am writing this letter to you" -- Miss Woods -- "with the hope that you will have the President see the two attachments. My wife is a cousin of Edward Haakinson, and many members of my family live in Sebring. I have been there many times over the past fifty years and am so proud that such a distinguished lady as you came from that town."

That is Sebring, Ohio.

"I retired from the Treasury Department as of 12-31-65. My position was 'super supervisor' in charge of sensitive audits -- one being you know who. I immediately took charge and verified the original audit as 'no change' and the case was sent back to Washington. Within a month it came back with a letter severely criticizing the N.C. report and referring to articles in the newspapers and magazines. I sent the case back to Washington with this comment: 'We don't work

HOOVER REPORTING CO., INC
320 Massachusetts Avenue, N.E.
Washington, D.C. 20002
(202) 546-6666

181

12

1 cases by what the news media and magazines say, we

2 base our findings on facts.' That settled the

3 case. Three times it had been sent to Los Angeles

4 from Washington."

5   Now, without saying who sent it, without saying it

6 was done with the knowledge of people high in government, it

7 was quite clear that the IRS was engaging in harassing

8 tactics during that campaign.

9   Now, that is what that refers to, the use of

10 their power in a personal way, the IRS, for harassment

11 purposes.

12   Now when we talk about using our power here, what

13 we are talking about, as far as I was concerned, having gone

14 through this agony, was not, in my view, to harass, but at

15 least to see what you gentlemen, as you stand before the bar

16 of history, must have in your minds, that you will be judged

17 not only by the very effective job you have done and are doing

18 on one side, but whether or not you have had a single standard

19 and are just as effective in going after any charges, the 140

20 that are before you right now, with regard to violations by

21 the other side.

22   It says here "contributors."

23 MR. HOROWITZ: I am sorry --

24 THE WITNESS: Let me finish the answer.

25   It says "contributors." That refers, of course,

182

13

to contributors to the other side.

"Larry O'Brien," and then his notes say, "Better they drop him now because" -- I don't know what the note means. It possibly means that I said on Larry O'Brien, don't go forward with him now because it would be too politically hot to do so.

Nevertheless, later on there is something to indicate that there is a suggestion that we go forward.

Then the next notation, "Check McGovern IRS files." Now this, understand, is Mr. Ehrlichman's notes. I should point out that I can never recall suggesting Mr. McGovern, Senator McGovern's files be checked. What I do recall is only a suggestion that the McGovern contributors might be checked.

BY MR. HOROWITZ:

Q. So, if I understand, sir, when you discussed using "our powers," that was to use the powers in the White House to get the Internal Revenue Service to audit Mr. O'Brien, is that right?

A. You are putting words in my mouth there that I did not say. What I am saying is, and I am looking at these notes -- I am refreshing my recollection about an event that occurred two years, three years ago, when I was engaged in activities that in my view were far more important than this type of activity, and from the notes and from my recollection

HOOVER REPORTING CO., INC.
320 Massachusetts Avenue, N.E.
Washington, D.C. 20002
(202) 546-6666

14

and to the best of my recollection, I can only say that I was suggesting that in the campaign that we should be as effective in conducting our investigations as they had been effective in conducting their investigations.

Q.   Now, sir, on the --

A.   As you noted, it says "Better they drop him now," whatever that means.

Q.   I was just about to ask you, sir, you indicated that you don't recall that. Do you believe that that was a discussion about talking to the Democratic Party or someone representing the Democratic Party and urging that they drop him, meaning that they drop Mr. O'Brien?

A.   You know, many times, Mr. Horowitz, people think that a President of the United States running for re-election, with a good chance to be re-elected, has a great deal of power, but even the suggestion that I or one of my representatives could have influence within the Democratic Party to get them to drop their National Chairman is so absurd that really I am not going to dignify it with a comment.

Q.   So, clearly, it doesn't mean that, it doesn't have anything to --

A.   I have answered the question.

Q.   If I might, if I could refer your attention to the second page of these notes, and the notes read, "Sh," and I believe that that is a reference to then Secretary Treasury

HOOVER REPORTING CO., INC.
320 Massachusetts Avenue, N.E.
Washington, D.C. 20002
(202) 546-6666

184

Shultz, and the three entries underneath that in Mr. Ehrlichman's handwriting are, "Must be political, give him an
external type, e.g., Larry O'Brien, check his returns."

Now, can you tell us about that part of the conversation?

A. Oh, I have no independent recollection of that
conversation.

Q. In connection with the phrase, "an external type,"
do you have any recollection of a conversation about convey-
ing to Mr. Shultz some bit of information concerning Mr.
O'Brien?

A. I have no recollection of telling Mr. Ehrlichman
what to do, except to be sure that since there was,
apparently, an investigation of the Hughes organization
involving O'Brien that it could be followed to its conclusion,
and as one of the later documents I trust you will put into
evidence will show, I tell them if nothing turns up, drop it.

You have that document, I assume?

Q. I think we will get to a document which reflects
that, sir.

A. Yes, and of course exculpatory matters should be
put in as well as others.

Q. If I just might have one more question on that.

A. You can have five.

Q. The words "external type," that doesn't bring

87

185

16

1 back any recollection of a conversation in which information

2 was conveyed in a fashion from some third party or something

3 of that nature, rather than directly from a White House

4 person to the IRS?

5   A.   I wouldn't know who such a third party would be.

6   Q.   Now, sir, at about this same time, as I have

7 alluded to, the Internal Revenue Service was in the process of

8 investigating all of these many Hughes related items and

9 they had come upon the O'Brien business and they had shortly,

10 prior to the time of this meeting to which we have been

11 referring, scheduled an interview of Mr. O'Brien and Mr.

12 O'Brien had failed to show up for that interview and there

13 was considerable discussion concerning that fact at the high

14 ranks of the Internal Revenue Service, and what I am asking

15 you --

16   A.   You are telling me you know this?

17   Q.   Right, that the evidence has established that.

18   A.   Okay.

19   Q.   And since that event crystallized shortly before

20 this meeting, can you tell us whether you became aware at or

21 about this time that such an event had occurred, i.e., they

22 had gone out to interview O'Brien and he hadn't shown up and

23 they were considering what next to do with him?

24   A.   You would have to refresh my recollection as to

25 some document on that. I am sure you have documents.

186

17

Q   All right, we will get to some documents.

A   Perhaps it would help to refresh my recollection if you would tell me, when you say that the IRS was having discussions with regard to whether to go forward with the O'Brien investigation -- is that what you are telling me?

Q   Well, exactly how to proceed next insofar as Mr. O'Brien was concerned in the context of their overall Hughes investigation, because to be sure Mr. O'Brien was one of probably hundreds of people --

A   What were your discussions, is what I am trying to get at.

Q   When next to schedule an interview and that type of thing.

A   When or whether, or both?

Q   Well, both to a certain extent.

A   You mean the Internal Revenue Service was not going forward, necessarily?

Q   Well, I think we will come back to that, but their policy at that time was to, as to a number of figures, both Republican and Democratic, that came up in the Hughes investigation --

A   That was not to use their --

Q   Mindful of the political sensitivity to try to delay it, but if I can go on I think we will come back to that.

89

187

18

1   A.   Not to do what they had done to me in '52 and in

2   '62?

3   Q.   I can't speak to that.

4   A.   Well, I have spoken to that.

5   Q.   At the same time, and perhaps related to the

6   notations on Mr. Ehrlichman's notes, and maybe you better

7   pull them back in front of you, the notation "contributors,"

8   about the same time as you are having this discussion with

9   Mr. Haldeman and Mr. Ehrlichman, evidence before the Grand

10   Jury establishes that there was discussion between Mr.

11   Ehrlichman and Mr. Chotiner about the production of a list

12   of contributors.

13   Now, we are not interested in that as an independent

14   matter, but we are interested in raising that because it seems

15   to tie in to the O'Brien matter, and what I would like to do

16   is place before you a list which will be marked D-2 --

17   A.   D-3. I got 2.

18   Q.   I am sorry, what I will mark as D-3, and ask you

19   to take a look at that.

20   (The document referred to

21   was marked Exhibit D-3

22   for identification.)

23   THE WITNESS: Yes.

24   What is your question, Mr. Horowitz?

25

188

19

BY MR. HOROWITZ:

Q.   In connection with the same conversation you had, sir, about Mr. O'Brien, which is reflected here in these notes of August 3, and the notation immediately above that "contributors," do you recall whether there was a discussion about using your powers against Democratic contributors? And I show you that list because it was a list, the evidence establishes, which was produced at about this period of time or following this period of time.

A.   Are these Democratic contributors?

Q.   Yes.

A.   Did you establish that?

Q.   Yes.

    Do you recall whether that was discussed, using your powers against contributors?

A.   I don't understand the question.

    Why don't you put it more precisely, so that the Grand Jury will be able to understand it when they read the transcript?

Q.   Perhaps I have confused you somewhat because it is a little premature to show you the list.

    The list was not produced until somewhat later but all I am asking you is on your notes, rather Mr. Ehrlichman's notes of this conversation with you, which is reflected in D-1, you referred to using our powers against contributors

HOOVER REPORTING CO., INC.
320 Massachusetts Avenue, N.E.
Washington, D.C. 20002
(202) 546-6666

189

20

1   and Larry O'Brien.

2   Now, in fact, the evidence establishes that the

3   same day as this meeting there was a meeting between-- Shall

4   I wait until you are finished consulting?

5   A.   Well, I think you are putting an assumption in

6   there that I do not say, "to use our powers against the

7   Democrats."

8   What we are referring to here is what I referred

9   to yesterday, and what I referred to again today, referred

10   to, Mr. Ruth, again today is something I strongly believe in,

11   that there should be a single standard where justice is

12   concerned and a single standard where government generally

13   is concerned, and not a double standard.

14   And I was quite aware that the IRS was harassing,

15   if I may use that term, not only contributors, but other

16   friends on our side. I felt that they should simply have a

17   single standard. That is what I was talking about.

18   I don't recall asking anybody to prepare a list

19   of contributors and give it to the IRS. I have no recollec-

20   tion of that. I have no recollection of seeing this list.

21   I think this was shown to me yesterday, maybe one of the

22   same lists was shown to me yesterday.

23   Q.   Sir, if I might continue on.

24   A.   Sure.

25   MR. HOROWITZ: We will mark as D-4, and I will

190

hand a copy to you, a slightly longer than one page typed

memorandum which bears the heading, "Memorandum for H. R.

Haldeman from The President."

I would like to ask you some questions about that.

THE WITNESS: Sure.

MR. HOROWITZ: That is Exhibit D-4.

(The document referred to

was marked Exhibit D-4

for identification.)

BY MR. HOROWITZ:

Q. You have taken the time to read this and I think

we had supplied this to you earlier. I want to ask you some

questions about several of the references there, to what

appears to have been a conversation between yourself and then

former Secretary Connally. I think he already had left his

position as Secretary of the Treasury.

The notes read, sir, and I am taking portions of

them, but by reference to your conversation about Mr. O'Brien

that, quote, "Connally feels very strongly that any informa-

tion we get in this matter should not be held but should pop

out just as quickly as possible."

And in the same vein you refer to, quote,

"Connally's very strong conviction is that dropping something

on O'Brien will have far more effect now than at a later

time," close quote.

HOOVER REPORTING CO., INC.
320 Massachusetts Avenue, N.E.
Washington, D.C. 20002
(202) 546-6666

191

22

1   Now, can you tell us what you intended to do in

2 that connection?

3   A.   All I can tell you is that I am reflecting here, as

4 I read this memorandum, what former Secretary Connally had

5 urged in terms of the handling of this matter.

6   Q.   Did you agree with his urging at the time?

7   A.   Let us speak very precise. In terms of a political

8 campaign, there are those who use broad and sweeping terms

9 which may mean one thing to them and something else to some-

10 body else.

11   As far as I was concerned, and obviously you will

12 put this in the record, I wanted the matter to be handled in

13 an evenhanded way.

14   For example, as you will note, I say "Ehrlichman

15 says that unless O'Brien responds with a request that he

16 submit to a voluntary IRS interrogation, that he be subpoenaed.

17 I think this should not be handled on that basis until at

18 least a telephone call is made by the head of the IRS to

19 O'Brien and before he stonewalls it, a subpoena should

20 follow."

21   That was the proper way to handle the Chairman of

22 the Democratic Party, rather than the way that Mr. Stans is

23 being handled by some of his opponents.

24   Q.   I am sorry, if I might just ask a few more

25 questions about this memorandum.

HOOVER REPORTING CO., INC.
320 Massachusetts Avenue, N.E.
Washington, D.C. 20002
(202) 546-6666

193

23

A.   Sure.

Q   You will note that in the beginning of the second paragraph on the first page, you refer to "Connally strongly urged that in addition to following through on the ▭ that was paid to O'Brien and associates, and the ▭ that was paid to Joe Napolitan, we should follow on the Napolitan returns in 1968 and O'Brien's as well," close quote.

Can you tell us whether Mr. Connally gave you that specific information or whether you gave it to him?

A.   I knew nothing about Mr. Napolitan or what had happened in the '68 campaign.

Back there, Connally, Mr. Connally was on the other side in '68, as you may recall, and he was supporting Mr. Humphrey and therefore what he points out, and if you read this memorandum, it says according to Connally there was approximately nine million dollars in unpaid bills after Humphrey's unsuccessful campaign. All of the bills submitted to Napolitan were paid. The others were not, apparently.

O'Brien at that time was making a great deal out of the fact he was an unpaid National Chairman. Of course, Connally was pointing up, I assume, from his experience on the Democratic side some of the matters that were popping up in the Hughes investigation that, if they proved to be true, should be publicly exposed.

193

24

1   Q   Just going back, because I perhaps lumped two

2 things into one in my question to you. Specifically, as far

3 as the information about [   ] paid to O'Brien and associ-

4 ates and [   ] that was paid to Napolitan, that particular

5 information, do you recall whether you conveyed that to Mr.

6 Connally or whether he conveyed that to you?

7   A   I have no recollection. I think that it was the

8 other way around, that Mr. Connally knew about it.

9   Q   Do you recall learning where Mr. Connally found

10 that out from?

11   A   No, I don't know where he could have learned it.

12 It could have very well been public knowledge at the time

13 of the Hughes investigation. In fact, be sure to check Jack

14 Anderson's column. Your staff seems to be very interested

15 in that, and that is always a good source.

16   Q   Sir, if I can continue on with this matter --

17   A   I won't ever stop you.

18   Q   (Continuing) -- beyond those notes, but let me

19 ask you first, can you tell us whether you had discussed

20 the O'Brien matter in the summer of '72 with Mr. Connally

21 prior to the time of what appears to have been an August 9,

22 '72, conversation?

23   A   I have no such recollection of a conversation, no.

24   Q   Do you recall having further conversations with

25 Mr. Connally later in the summer regarding the same business

25

1 of Mr. O'Brien's tax situation?

2   A.   No, I have no independent recollection of any

3 further conversation with Mr. Connally.

4   Q.   Either telephonic or in a meeting?

5   A.   No. No.

6   Oh, I would have to qualify that to this extent:

7 When nothing, as I had expected, developed out of the O'Brien

8 investigation, and instead of conducting two years of

9 harassment against him, as they have against Mr. Rebozo, for

10 example, they simply dropped the matter.

11   I remember that on one occasion -- that was

12 shortly before the election -- Connally said that IRS, he

13 says that is what you have to expect, I didn't expect they

14 would do anything. He said they are right in the pocket, at

15 that time at least, in the pocket of the Democratic Party.

16   I would say the top leadership was all supporters

17 of McGovern. I think that was the other point he made. I

18 am not referring to the man at the very top because, as you

19 know, there are only two people appointed by the President,

20 with the advice of the Secretary of Treasury.

21   All of the rest is a self-perpetuating bureaucracy

22 and it was that bureaucracy that Connally, even as Secretary

23 of Treasury, was unable to control, and I don't mean control

24 for improper purposes but to control them to get them to have

25 a single standard, the same thing I am urging upon all of you.

HOOVER REPORTING CO., INC.
320 Massachusetts Avenue, N.E.
Washington, D.C. 20002
(202) 546-6666

195

26

1   Q.   I understand that.

2   If I might continue on and fill in a few facts

3   which evidence before the Grand Jury has established.

4   In mid-August, in fact, the Internal Revenue

5   Service arranged an interview with Mr. O'Brien, and they did

6   interview Mr. O'Brien, and it is of interest to the Grand

7   Jury whether you received, personally received, any memorandum

8   prepared by the Internal Revenue Service, one or another of

9   their agents, concerning or summarizing that interview.

10   A.   I don't recall personally receiving any memoranda.

11   I do recall receiving a report that the investigation was a

12   dry hole and that the whole matter was being dropped at some

13   point. I don't know who gave it to me.

14   Q.   We will get to that in a minute, sir, but just for

15   the time being if we can distinguish between just a memorandum

16   of an interview of O'Brien, and you indicated you don't

17   recall receiving such a memorandum --

18   A.   I say I don't recall receiving any memoranda on

19   the matter. I am telling you what I do recall and what I

20   know the Grand Jury is most interested in is what happened in

21   all of this case, and what happened was that the IRS conducted

22   a cursory investigation and dropped the matter and we did

23   nothing further.

24   Incidentally, we put nothing out publicly on it.

25   Q.   As far as the memorandum of the interview, you

HOOVER REPORTING CO., INC.
320 Massachusetts Avenue, N.E.
Washington, D.C. 20002
(202) 546-6666

27

196

don't recall having seen one. Do you recall Mr. Ehrlichman
or anyone else briefing you or discussing with you those
things that Mr. O'Brien had said during his interview?

A.   I don't have any recollection of that. I think
it would depend on the time, Mr. Horowitz. If I were busy
with, you know, preparing a speech or something of that sort,
they wouldn't have briefed me on a matter of this sort.

Normally, even though this was the campaign
period, at that time we, as you know, were rather busy in
international affairs, and I simply wasn't paying much
attention to the campaign, and I left it to my top appointees
to handle matters of this sort. But I am not saying that he
may not have briefed me. He might have.

Q.   Now, the interview and any conversations about
the interview would have occurred in mid-August, and of
course the convention at which you were nominated again was
August 21 or 23 -- something in that neighborhood.

Now, thereafter, certain reports, in late August
and early September, were prepared by the Internal Revenue
Service which discuss and analyze Mr. O'Brien's situation.

Now, you have alluded to one, and I would like
to mark as the next Grand Jury --

A.   I haven't alluded to any written report that I
have seen. I have told you, Mr. Horowitz, that I have no
recollection of having seen a written report on this, no

HOOVER REPORTING CO., INC.
320 Massachusetts Avenue, N.E.
Washington, D.C. 20002
(202) 546-6666

197

28

1 recollection. I may have -- I may have. It may have crossed

2 my desk. I do recall having received in substance a report

3 that nothing was developed on the O'Brien investigation, it

4 has been dropped.

5   MR. HOROWITZ: If I might, sir, let me mark as

6 D-5, a report which was prepared by the Internal Revenue

7 Service.

8   THE WITNESS: For whom?

9   MR. HOROWITZ: I will give that to you.

10   This one was an Internal Report prepared to the

11 Commissioner from the Acting Assistant Commissioner.

12   (The document referred to

13   was marked Exhibit D-5

14   for identification.)

15   THE WITNESS: I have scanned the report.

16   BY MR. HOROWITZ:

17   Q.   You have scanned that, and do you recall that or

18 anything substantially similar to that, recall having seen

19 it, Mr. Nixon?

20   Q.   I don't recall. It is possible in the mass of

21 material that comes across a president's desk that it might

22 have been sent to me, if it was available to us. And,

23 incidentally, so that we can be perfectly candid, this was

24 one of those sensitive case reports where it would have been

25 available to us, so I assume it was available to somebody.

HOOVER REPORTING CO., INC.
320 Massachusetts Avenue, N.E.
Washington, D.C. 20002
(202) 546-6666

198

29

1   Q   Let me ask you this: Do you recall Mr. Ehrlichman

2 informing you around this period of time that he had himself

3 personally, and not yourself, that he had received reports

4 similar to that?

5   A   No, I only recall that Mr. Ehrlichman was follow-

6 ing the O'Brien matter. He didn't indicate to me that I can

7 recall what reports, if any, he was receiving in written

8 form or oral form. And he certainly wouldn't have wasted my j

9 time by going into great detail about a matter of this sort.

10   All that I recall with regard to Mr. Ehrlichman,

11 my conversation with him about this matter at that time, is

12 what I already testified to, that the Internal Revenue

13 Service has completed its investigation of O'Brien, and have

14 found nothing. And I said, well, that is what I expected,

15 drop it, they won't try to find anything.

16   Q   Sir, some evidence before the Grand Jury

17 establishes that Mr. Ehrlichman was, during this period of

18 time, in contact with a Mr. Roger Barth, who was a gentleman

19 who was then employed by the Internal Revenue Service as

20 Assistant to the Commissioner, and that at one time or

21 another during this period the two of them discussed this

22 matter.

23   Do you recall being aware of Mr. Barth and/or

24 aware of Mr. Ehrlichman's contact with Mr. Barth on the

25 subject?

HOOVER REPORTING CO., INC.
320 Massachusetts Avenue, N.E.
Washington, D.C. 20002
(202) 546-6666

199

30

1
2
3
4
5
6
7
8
9
10
11
12
13
14
15
16
17
18
19
20
21
22
23
24
25

A.   I was aware of Mr. Barth, although I don't know him well, I was aware that he was working in IRS, and from the documents that you have shown me it appears that Mr. Barth and Mr. Ehrlichman were in contact, but I have no recollection of it independent of those documents.

Q.   All right, that was my question.

A.   Sorry for such a long answer.

Q.   Nor do you recall whether Mr. Barth-- Let me rephrase that.

Do you recall understanding or hearing at that point of time that Mr. Barth had prepared some report?

A.   I don't recall that. It is possible that I might have been so told.

Q.   Now, sir, I have asked you about reports. There is a notation on another document -- I think I can just handle this with one question really -- which leads me to ask you whether you during this period of time, you yourself saw Mr. O'Brien's tax returns?

A.   That I saw his tax returns?

Q.   Or asked to see his tax returns, yes.

A.   I can say categorically that I did not see his tax returns, and as far as asking to see his tax returns, I can't recall asking to see his tax returns.

I didn't even take, as I pointed out yesterday, enough time looking at my own returns, let alone looking at

HOOVER REPORTING CO., INC.
320 Massachusetts Avenue, N.E.
Washington, D.C. 20002
(202) 546-6666

200

31

1   somebody else's.

2   MR. HOROWITZ: Now if I might mark as D-6, what

3   are handwritten notes, again Mr. Ehrlichman is the author of

4   the notes, and they are dated, although the date is not

5   complete here but we have established that the date is

6   September 5, 1972, and they relate to a conversation aboard

7   Air Force One between yourself and Mr. Ehrlichman and there

8   are some notations there, and I would like to ask you about

9   those.

10   (The document referred to

11   was marked Exhibit D-6

12   for identification.)

13   THE WITNESS: Have you previously shown us this

14   document or is this a new one?

15   MR. HOROWITZ: No, no, you have seen all of these.

16   These were all furnished to you.

17   THE WITNESS: When they are new, if you will let

18   me know, I will read them more carefully.

19   MR. HOROWITZ: Well, they haven't been.

20   THE WITNESS: That is perfectly all right for you

21   to have any you have got.

22   Go ahead with your question.

23   BY MR. HOROWITZ:

24   Q   Now, sir, at the bottom of this first page it

25   reads, "6. Anonymous to Hart re Hughes and O'Brien, warn

201

32

1 Senator McGovern," and McGovern is abbreviated.

2   Now, do you recall having a conversation with Mr.

3 Ehrlichman or this conversation with Mr. Ehrlichman about

4 warning Senator McGovern about the O'Brien-Hughes business?

5   A.   This is what date?

6   Q.   This is September 5, 1972.

7   A.   I have no recollection of the conversation and it

8 is very hard for me to decipher Mr. Ehrlichman's notes due

9 to the fact that he, like many note-takers, has a practice

10 of writing notes to himself as well as recording what he is

11 hearing. All that I say is that I don't recall any conver-

12 sation of this kind.

13   Q.   Merely in an effort to refresh your recollection,

14 do you have a recollection of a conversation with Mr.

15 Ehrlichman that McGovern should be informed that there was

16 this material pertaining to O'Brien's tax situation which

17 could prove to be embarrassing to McGovern or to the

18 Democrats?

19   A.   No, I do not have a recollection of this, apart

20 from what these notes show.

21   I, frankly, would be very surprised, very sur-

22 prised, if I indicated that we were going to try to warn

23 Senator McGovern -- apparently the Hart referred to is now

24 the young man who is now a Senator from Colorado, and Miss

25 Westwood, you know, I guess she was the chairman of their

202

33

campaign -- that you better do something about O'Brien.

What difference would it have made? I don't understand what this is about.

Q.   One final question on that. I phrased my question in terms of Mr. Ehrlichman.

Do you recall any conversations with anyone around that period of time which pertain to that type of subject, that is, informing the Democrats of this?

A.   I don't recall any conversations of this nature at that time. I cannot affirm or deny that people working in the campaign, like Mr. Ehrlichman, may have brought up subjects, some of them as far out as this one. It seems far out today.

Q.   But you don't remember him bringing up that far-out-type thing?

A.   No. It sure wasn't my idea. I think it was a stupid idea, frankly.

Q.   On the second page, sir, there are the two sentences, or two notations to which I have not yet alluded which appear there: "Get someone in Las Vegas. Do it. Ask how much he got."

And there is other evidence, sir, that Mr. Ehrlichman and/or Mr. Barth had someone from the Internal Revenue Service situated in Las Vegas, apparently, to get information.

105

203

34

1 Do you recall hearing anything like that or knowing

2 anything about that?

3 A. Until these papers were put in front of me, I had

4 no recollection of that. Having read these notes and also

5 the transcript of a telephone call that Mr. Ehrlichman had

6 with Mr. Shultz and I think the then head of the Internal

7 Revenue Service, apparently there was somebody, they had

8 somebody in Las Vegas, but I am not testifying to that on

9 firsthand knowledge. That is simply hearsay.

10 Q. I understand that.

11 Did you know that Mr. Ehrlichman had anyone from

12 the Internal Revenue Service who was, in effect, acting out

13 of channels for him in the fashion that is suggested by

14 those notes, that he had someone in Las Vegas?

15 A. No. What I know is what his notes show.

16 Q. Now, --

17 A. As far as his notes are concerned, I am not going

18 to testify to their veracity and I am not going to testify as

19 to their interpretation, because I don't know what he meant

20 by them.

21 Q. Now, finally, Mr. Nixon, I think we are at the end

22 of our documents and drawing to a close here, but let me show

23 you what we will mark as D-7, which are, again, Mr. Ehrlich-

24 man's handwritten notes of a meeting between yourself and him,

25 and again part of the date appears to have been cut off, but

204

35

1 we have established that it was September 30, 1972.

2 I would like you to-- This again is something

3 you have seen before, but I will place it before you.

4 (The document referred to

5 was marked Exhibit D-7

6 for identification.)

7 THE WITNESS: You also have-- Would you please

8 give me the memoranda I wrote to Haldeman? You want to put

9 those two in evidence, don't you?

10 MR. HOROWITZ: I believe that is in evidence, sir.

11 THE WITNESS: I don't see them. I have one.

12 There are two to Haldeman. Could I see the second one or

13 the first one?

14 MR. HOROWITZ: We can get into that.

15 THE WITNESS: No, I want to see them. I mean I

16 should be able to see them. You furnished them to us earlier

17 MR. HOROWITZ: Let's mark that D-8, and that is a

18 one-page typewritten memorandum for H. R. Haldeman from The

19 President, dated August 9, 1972.

20 THE WITNESS: Could I see that too, because it

21 may refresh my recollection.

22 (The document referred to

23 was marked Exhibit D-8

24 for identification.)

25 THE WITNESS: Just in answering your question,

HOOVER REPORTING CO., INC.
320 Massachusetts Avenue, N.E.
Washington, D.C. 20002
(202) 546-6666

205

36

the memorandum to Mr. Haldeman on August 9, with regard to this whole matter, and which counsel has not questioned me on yet, says on both the O'Brien and Kimmelman matters -- Kimmelman, incidentally, was the finance secretary of the McGovern campaign -- "I want you personally to follow up and keep me posted on what has developed. Of course if nothing turns up, drop the whole matter. But let's be sure we have gone the extra mile and developed material before we drop the matter."

I think, Mr. Ruth, it is proper to have that in and be questioned on that as well as matters that are derogatory, do you not?

MR. RUTH: I think Mr. Horowitz intended to.

THE WITNESS: Well, Mr. Horowitz didn't intend to put this in thoroughly and I have.

MR. RUTH: I think he intended to put it in.

THE WITNESS: I don't question Mr. Horowitz' ethics. I am sure he was going to put it in.

Now, what do you want to know about this one?

BY MR. HOROWITZ:

Q.   By this one-- I think we have confused some pieces of paper in --

A.   This is September 30, '72.

Q.   On the bottom of the second page, we have the notes, "Larry O'Brien - worry him."

206

37

1   What was that a reference to?

2   A.   What is this conversation, please?

3   Q.   This is a conversation between Ehrlichman and

4   yourself.

5   A.   Well, as I say, three years later all I can

6   imagine is that Larry O'Brien was worrying Mr. Stans with a

7   lawsuit. He was certainly being a very effective-- Mr.

8   McGovern made a great mistake in not using him. He was the

9   only effective pro that McGovern had working for him and was

10   worrying us. So I think there must have been some discussion

11   of worrying Mr. O'Brien with regard to the fact that he,

12   having claimed that he was an unpaid chairman now apart from

13   the IRS investigation, had received in the neighborhood of

14   two hundred thousand dollars a year from the Howard Hughes

15   organization.

16   I thought that would worry him, and I thought it

17   was perfectly proper to put that out.

18   Q.   You understood, sir, did you not, that those

19   funds had been paid, at least as far as the IRS investigation

20   had been established, had been paid for his services. They

21   weren't paid as a salary for the Democratic National Commit-

22   tee.

23   A.   As far as the IRS investigation is concerned --

24   just a moment.

25   Mr. O'Brien, you understand, had made a point

HOOVER REPORTING CO., INC.
320 Massachusetts Avenue, N.E.
Washington, D.C. 20002
(202) 546-6666

109

38

1   that he was an unpaid national chairman when he was chairman

2   of the National Committee. By "unpaid National Chairman,"

3   that means to me and it would mean to members of the Grand

4   Jury that he is not going to be paid there and they don't

5   think he would be taking something on the side.

6   And the point was that the Howard Hughes organiza-

7   tion at that time was under intensive public investigation

8   as well as private, with regard to payoffs. That is how

9   the investigations began. And here Larry O'Brien had his

10   hand in the till there.

11   Now, I am putting now a connotation on it which

12   I do not want to be left in the record as being unfair to

13   O'Brien. It is very possible that his story about it is

14   correct, that he rendered enormous services for the Howard

15   Hughes organization even though he didn't register as a

16   lobbyist apparently for them, in doing the things that they

17   wanted to have done. And if he did, he was entitled to be

18   paid, that was all.

19   Q.   So let me understand.

20   Those facts you felt, in view of his puffing his

21   unpaid status, should be brought out to indicate that perhaps

22   he had not been unpaid, is that it?

23   A.   You know, you have to think of the campaign. In

24   the one sense our campaign, we were the campaign of the rich,

25   with all of the big people supporting us, and their campaign

208

39

1 was the campaign of the people, you know, like Mr. Strauss,

2 the Democratic National Chairman took fifty thousand dollars

3 in cash from Ashland Oil, and apparently sold somebody on

4 the idea that he didn't report it because he thought these

5 were five-dollar contributions from people who worked for

6 Ashland Oil that were against the war.

7   You couldn't find that many people in Kentucky

8 that were against the war at that time. And yet, it was

9 accepted.

10   In the case of O'Brien, this purist image of no

11 connection with big business, which the McGovern campaign

12 of course was trying to do, and, incidentally, no connection

13 with the milk interests, and we received twice as many

14 letters from Democratic Senators, including one from McGovern

15 and one from Humphrey, asking for ninety percent parity on

16 milk as we did from Republican Senators, and three times as

17 many from Democratic Congressmen as we did from Republicans,

18 and, incidentally, they were all proper, all proper.

19   Q.   I am sorry, sir, could I just turn back to the

20 O'Brien matter?

21   A.   Oh, all right.

22   Q.   On the following page, you state -- I am sorry,

23 Mr. Ehrlichman's notes state, "Get it to O'Brien. Don't

24 publish."

25   Does that refresh your recollection as to a

HOOVER REPORTING CO., INC.
320 Massachusetts Avenue, N.E.
Washington, D.C. 20002
(202) 546-6666

209

40

1   conversation in which the purpose was not to make public

2   these facts but rather to convey the information to O'Brien,

3   indicating that he did possibly face tax problems?

4   A.   No, it doesn't refresh my recollection. I don't

5   remember the conversations, the specifics of it.

6   I only remember, as I have indicated, my general

7   interest in the O'Brien matter due to the fact that he was

8   giving us a rough time, and I felt that we had, at least,

9   as I pointed out only if the facts bore it out, and we

10   should emphasize this. I said if nothing turns up, drop the

11   matter.

12   Now, that ought to be there -- the Grand Jury I

13   think is interested in a matter like that, as well as some-

14   thing which says if something doesn't turn up, go after

15   him anyway.

16   That is what I am trying to say, and I think you

17   should emphasize that to the Grand Jury too.

18   Q.   In the same conversation Mr. Ehrlichman's notes

19   read, and just for your reference I am on page 3, reads,

20   quote, "Bobby Baker blowing whistle on Larry O'Brien and

21   others," close quote. And immediately above that you have

22   "Gossip" -- I am sorry, I misspoke, Mr. Ehrlichman has

23   "Gossip - plant, Jack Anderson," and Jack Anderson was

24   underlined.

25   Did you have conversations at around this time

HOOVER REPORTING CO., INC.
320 Massachusetts Avenue, N.E.
Washington, D.C. 20002
(202) 546-6666

210

41

1 of planting this information with reporters?

2 A.   Since you have put in the record the name of

3 Bobby Baker, let me just be sure that after all of the abuse

4 that poor man has taken, and apparently some of it deserved,

5 but Bobby Baker had apparently talked to people in our

6 campaign, and when he saw that we were the victims of the

7 roughest campaign physically -- and incidentally, when we do

8 get into this business of wiretapping and so forth, I want to

9 be sure that the Special Prosecutor tells us what he has

10 done with regard to the bombing of our Phoenix headquarters,

11 what he has done with regard to twenty-five thousand dollars

12 in damage directly ordered by the McGovern Campaign --

13 Q.   Sir, I am sorry, but --

14 A.   All right, now we will come back to this.

15 Bobby Baker came in and said, look, he says I

16 have enough on O'Brien to sink him. He put that in.

17 Q.   Who did he tell that to?

18 A.   Who did he tell that to? He told it to somebody

19 and they reported it to me. I don't recall.

20 Q.   Do you remember who reported it to you?

21 A.   Who reported it to me? I think it could have

22 been Haldeman, that Bobby Baker was talking.

23 Q.   On these same notes, sir, on the last page there

24 is the notation, quote, "Via Andreas, dash" --

25 A.   Incidentally, Bobby Baker is reporting he was

211

42

1 going to blow the whistle, not only on Larry O'Brien, he

2 said, but a number of Democratic Senators that he, Bobby

3 Baker, personally had delivered cash to.

4 Apparently Bobby Baker had been a bagman for

5 Hughes at one time, as well, or at least a transmittal valve

6 for many others, as well, and he said there were a number of

7 Democratic Senators, technically those on the Left, that

8 were taking a sanctimonious attitude and that he wanted

9 all of this brought out.

10 Incidentally, nothing came of that. He would not

11 have been a credible man to use in a campaign, and that

12 kind of gossip I didn't frankly feel was proper.

13 Q   In other words, you do recall discussing using

14 the Bobby Baker information? Is that it?

15 A   We didn't use it. That is the whole point.

16 Q   You recall discussing it and deciding not to, is

17 that it?

18 A   I recall that it was brought to my attention, and

19 it seemed to me to be so way out that with Bobby Baker just

20 having finished a prison term, that it would be not right

21 to use it, and also I felt that we should just go on and

22 conduct our own campaign.

23 We were doing all right without that kind of

24 stuff. We allowed them to engage in that kind of thing, but

25 we went on and did our campaign without it.

HOOVER REPORTING CO., INC.
320 Massachusetts Avenue, N.E.
Washington, D.C. 20002
(202) 546-6666

212

43

1   Q.   On the last page there are the notations, quote,

2   "Via Andreas - worry O'Brien - work through Dean," and other

3   evidence before the Grand Jury establishes that there was

4   an attempt to have Mr. Andreas make an overture to Mr.

5   O'Brien, indicating that Mr. O'Brien was in tax trouble.

6   Do you recall a discussion about that, sir?

7   A.   I don't have an independent recollection of that.

8   I have seen these notes and I have been trying to think what

9   it must mean.

10   I can only surmise that what it may mean is that

11   Andreas first was a very big financial supporter of the

12   Democratic Party.

13   He was also one of our supporters in this campaign

14   and it was felt that Andreas, who also apparently was a

15   pretty good political operator, could have some influence

16   on O'Brien in terms of the violence and viciousness -- strike

17   the word "violence" -- in terms of the word "viciousness" of

18   the attacks that O'Brien was making, not only on Mr. Stans,

19   but on me.

20   Q.   Was it discussed that he would have more influ-

21   ence if O'Brien was told that O'Brien faced tax problems

22   otherwise?

23   A.   I don't recall that we talked about O'Brien -- I

24   don't recall any conversation about O'Brien's tax problems.

25   Q.   In other words, was Andreas to be a courier to

213

44

Mr. O'Brien to have an influence?

A.   I think probably this notation is more interesting here where it says "Offer him a retainer."

MR. HOROWITZ: All right, sir, just two or three more questions from Mr. Hecht.

BY MR. HECHT:

Q.   Aside from Mr. O'Brien's receipt of income from the Hughes Tool Company, were you aware that after the '68 campaign he had taken employment as an officer in a Wall Street brokerage firm?

A.   No, I really wasn't, not until it was brought to my attention in this investigation.

Q.   Were you aware that, jumping ahead in time, not the summer of '72 but in the spring of 1973, that Mr. O'Brien was audited, or an audit was begun as to the handling of some stocks that he had owned in that brokerage firm that he had been officer of and that he had taken a loss on those stocks?

A.   No. I am learning that, I think, for the first time right now.

All that I am aware of is that I understood from the papers that you have provided -- sorry, that we have provided you and you have provided me, that O'Brien after the '68 campaign wanted employment.

He went with a brokerage firm. The brokerage

HOOVER REPORTING CO., INC.
320 Massachusetts Avenue, N.E.
Washington, D.C. 20002
(202) 546-6666

45   214

1   firm went broke and that after that he went with Hughes, even

2   though Hughes, I think, had offered him a rather good job

3   before he went with the brokerage firm. He then decided to

4   go with the Hughes firm, which proved to be a very good

5   choice for him.

6   Q   Now, as to the receipt of funds by Mr. O'Brien

7   from the Hughes Tool Company or the stock loss issue or any

8   other issues on Mr. O'Brien's returns, did you have any

9   conversations directly with Mr. Shultz, who, during the

10 relevant period of time, was Secretary of the Treasury?

11   A   I have no recollection of any such conversations.

12 I don't believe Mr. Shultz would bring such technical, and

13 what to me would be picayune, matters to my attention. I

14 believe that all that would be brought to my attention by

15 Mr. Shultz or Mr. Ehrlichman, whoever was familiar with this,

16 the big issue, whether or not Mr. O'Brien was or was not

17 vulnerable to a major income tax violation. If he was, I

18 wanted to know.

19   Q   Did you have occasion to discuss that question

20 directly with Mr. Shultz that you recall?

21   A   No, not with Mr. Shultz that I can recall.

22   Q   Did you have occasion to discuss that matter with

23 the then Commissioner of the Internal Revenue Service,

24 Johnnie Walters?

25   A   Not that I can recall. I don't think I saw him

HOOVER REPORTING CO., INC.
320 Massachusetts Avenue, N.E.
Washington, D.C. 20002
(202) 546-6666

46   215

1   at all.

2   MR. HECHT: I think that covers our questions, but

3   we are going to take a short recess to inquire of the repre-

4   sentatives of the Grand Jury whether they have any further

5   questions.

6   THE WITNESS: I should have talked to Mr. Walters,

7   I guess.

8   (Short recess.)

9   MR. HOROWITZ: Sir, we have no further questions

10   for you.

11   Thank you.

12   THE WITNESS: Let me say, Mr. Horowitz, and Mr. --

13   MR. HECHT: Hecht.

14   THE WITNESS: I thought it was. H-e-c --

15   MR. HECHT: -- h-t.

16   THE WITNESS: I thought so.

17   That is the store in Washington?

18   MR. HECHT: Yes, sir. No relation.

19   THE WITNESS: Do you have a part --

20   MR. HECHT: Unfortunately not.

21   THE WITNESS: They do well, I think. We bought

22   a dining room set there once.

23   I did want to say for the record, and particularly

24   to Mr. Horowitz and Mr. Hecht, I know you have been living

25   with this O'Brien investigation and you have gone through a

47   216

lot of work to prepare these questions and you have probably

been somewhat, perhaps, disappointed that some of my answers

have been, well, to put it mildly, rather testy, which is

not my usual way of trying to answer questions in what is

basically a legal forum.

But I think that it is time, and perhaps the

Special Prosecutor, when he files his final report, will have

one paragraph in for history, it is time for us to recognize

that in politics in America, and this is not excusable, but

it does explain it to an extent, particularly where the

highest office in the land is involved, and even in some

instances where campaigns for governor in major states or

senators are involved, that in politics some pretty rough

tactics are used. We deplore them all.

I am very proud of the fact that as a result of

my orders, and I gave them directly, that never to my

knowledge was anybody in my campaign responsible for heckling

Mr. McGovern or shouting him down. Sometimes he was heckled,

not much. I told them not to do it.

Now, actually my decision was not all that

altruistic, to be quite honest. My decision was based on

the fact that I didn't think it would do any good. Why

martyr the poor fellow? He was having enough trouble.

And yet, there was not an appearance I made in

the campaign, not one in which not only we were the subject

48   217

1   of voice heckling through loud speakers and the rest. That

2   is why I got a little hoarse, even though I didn't make many

3   speeches -- but also of violence and threats of violence,

4   violence in San Francisco, for example, which I am sure you

5   have investigated or will. And if you are going back a few

6   years, you can pick up the violence in San Jose when a

7   direct assault was made on our car, and so forth.

8   What I am pointing out here is not that our

9   campaign was pure; what I am pointing out also is not that

10 theirs was all that bad, but what I am saying is that having

11 been in politics for the last twenty-five years, that politics

12 is a rough game, and in 1952, as I said, I was subjected

13 to some of the most brutal assaults, not only by the IRS and

14 political opponents, but particularly by some elements of

15 the press.

16   Now, I have given out some too, to be perfectly

17 honest -- I am speaking now of speeches and that sort of

18 thing.

19   But in 1962, the same thing, where the Administra-

20 tion in power, and they were pretty smart, I guess, rather

21 than using a group of amateur Watergate bugglers -- burglars

22 -- well, they were bunglers -- used the FBI, used the IRS,

23 and used it directly by their own orders against, in one

24 instance, a man who had been Vice President of the United

25 States, running for Governor, and in another instance a man

HOOVER REPORTING CO., INC.
320 Massachusetts Avenue, N.E.
Washington, D.C. 20002
(202) 546-6666

120

218

49

1 running for President of the United States, the FBI, accord-

2 ing to information that we have, were at least ordered to,

3 and whether they did it or not, I can't say, to bug the

4 plane of the Presidential candidate.

5 What I am simply saying is that here we must be

6 under no illusions about what happens in politics in

7 America. I don't condone it.

8 I see memoranda which I have long forgotten.

9 What really counts in the long run is what happens, and when

10 I see this long list -- this is what they call the enemy

11 list -- what happened? Nothing.

12 I never recall seeing any income tax return; I

13 never recall seeing any result of any of this done. What

14 happened to Mr. O'Brien's case? Nothing.

15 A cursory, pleasant interview with the IRS. That

16 is one thing. All that I say is that the Special Prosecutor,

17 you had your job, you had to do it, we made our mistakes,

18 we have to pay for them.

19 All have paid a heavy price. I am paying mine,

20 but if there is one thing I am going to do to the day I die,

21 it is going to be to insist to the best of my ability that

22 whether it is the case of political leaders or the press,

23 including the television people, or education leaders, that

24 it is time where ethics are concerned in politics, not to

25 clean up one side and then turn your back and forget what

HOOVER REPORTING CO., INC.
320 Massachusetts Avenue, N.E.
Washington, D.C. 20002
(202) 546-6666

219

50

1   happens on the other side.

2   I would say that our campaigns in '68 and in 1972,

3   in terms of what we did, were clean campaigns. I would say

4   as far as their campaigns were concerned, there was some

5   violence, there was some rough heckling, but we took it.

6   And I am confident that Mr. McGovern, who I

7   understand is a rather gentle man, probably wouldn't have

8   approved it, just as I wouldn't have approved any violence,

9   but it happened.

10   But I simply want the record to show here that

11 when you conduct this extensive investigation of whether or

12 not Mr. Larry O'Brien was being persecuted by the Administra-

13 tion in power, I think, and I don't urge you to do this

14 because now he has a splendid position and I think he is the

15 Basketball Commissioner, and he deserves it. He doesn't

16 have any money and he has a big family, and I think he is a

17 decent guy actually, but he plays politics tough.

18   But if you were to look, as Bobby Baker suggested,

19 into Larry O'Brien's activities politically over the years,

20 and into the activities of some of the Democratic Senators

21 and others, including some Republicans who are taking this

22 sanctimonious attitude about the cleanliness of their

23 campaigns, if you would put them to the same test you have

24 put us, you would find that we come out rather well.

25   I don't say this, as I say finally, in

220

51 1 justification of any wrongdoing where it occurred. I deplore

2 it. I regret it. And I am paying a price for it.

3 And as far as you gentlemen are concerned, you have

4 your job to do, and I respect you for doing it. For two years

5 you have been on this job; for two years, and you have been

6 working very, very hard to expose anything that we did that

7 was wrong.

8 And I do not, in what I am writing at the present

9 time, my memoirs, which I hope will come out before you die

10 or before I die, I am not going to be critical of the fact

11 that you are doing the job you are hired to do.

12 But I am going to come down hard, and you, I would

13 urge, thinking not of yourselves because at the present time,

14 if I could give one last bit of advice, taking the double

15 standard is going to make you much more popular with the

16 Washington press corps, with the Georgetown social set, if you

17 ever go to Georgetown, with the power elite in this country,

18 but, on the other hand, think of your children -- they are

19 going to judge you in the pages of history and as they look

20 at you, they are going to say, well, now, you did a pretty

21 good job one way, but did they overlook other things because

22 they believed things.

23 I mean I am not unaware of the fact that the great

24 majority of the people working in the Special Prosecutor's

25 Office did not support me for President. After all, there

HOOVER REPORTING CO., INC.
320 Massachusetts Avenue, N.E.
Washington, D.C. 20002
(202) 546-6666

221

52

1   are many millions of people who didn't -- about thirty-

2   eight percent of the people in the country. I respect

3   those who didn't, just as I am thankful for those who did

4   support me.

5   I am not unaware of the fact, too, that therefore

6   you would have a motive to go after me and my associates

7   and to ignore others, but I also say I just trust in the

8   future, as you go on, after you leave these positions, have

9   a single standard. That is what the country needs.

10   I am sorry to take so much time.

11   MR. RUTH: I wonder if we could recess a second

12 because the Prosecutors are not allowed to respond to the

13 charge of being partisan; we are not going to respond, and

14 we will pick up in the area of questioning having to do

15 with the wiretaps in a couple of minutes.

16   THE WITNESS: Sorry, I intended no personal

17 reflection.

18   (Short recess.)

19

20

21

22

23

24

25

HOOVER REPORTING CO., INC.
320 Massachusetts Avenue, N.E.
Washington, D.C. 20002
(202) 546-6666

Notes

Page

1   A corollary to the *5 W's and the H* is how to cover any sort of an accident. If there are fatalities, they come first, at the top of the article; by name if available and appropriate (minors are often not identified by name in news articles). Then the injured and then property damage. If there are no fatalities, then the injured are described first. If there are no fatalities or injured, then property damage is described first, at the top of the article.

        Facts in news articles are described in descending importance; journalists call this the Inverted Pyramid, or upside-down pyramid. Minor details trail off to the bottom of the article; to the bottom of the Inverted Pyramid. To save space on the page a 10-inch article (in column form) could be cut (from the bottom up) to an eight-inch article and readers would not notice (or care about) the loss of two inches of minor material from the bottom.

1   Airliner crash ... months later .... On August 31, 1988, Delta flight 1141 crashed on take-off at the Dallas-Fort Worth airport. There were nine fatalities and 96 survivors of the accident. It was one of the worst airline disasters of the year. The airliner skidded, broke into two parts and burst into flames. It was called the "dead goose" disaster, as the cockpit broke sideways upon impact. The conclusion: after major investigations, which lasted almost a full year, Delta concluded that the crew did not set the aircraft's flaps correctly for take-off, which caused the crash. The flight crew was fired. The Associated Press, which covered the story extensively throughout the months, filed its last article July 19, 1989. See Thomas Fensch, *Associated Press Coverage of a Major Disaster: The Crash of Delta Flight 1141.* (Hillsdale, N.J.: Lawrence Erlbaum Publishers, 1989).

1-2   "Richard Nixon led the United States ..." Weiner, *One Man Against the World*, pp. 1-2.

2   Family names and deaths, Wikipedia, Nixon biography.

2-3   Nixon's father and mother, in Weiner, pp. 313.

3   ... called his last speech "pathetic," in Weiner, pp. 312.

3   Nixon's Father, in Wikipedia entry, Francis A. Nixon.

4   Navy service, Wikipedia entry, Richard Nixon.

5   Political career, Wikipedia entry, Richard Nixon.

6   "Tricky Dick," Wikipedia entry, Richard Nixon.

8   ... last press conference, in Aitken, Jonathan, *Nixon: A Life*, pp. 304-305.

8   "silent majority" in www.history.com and elsewhere.

9   "... building outhouses in Peoria," Weiner, pp. 55.

9   "The president spent far more ..." Weiner, pp. 56.

13   "(Charles) Colson, whose office had ..." Dean, *Blind Ambition*, pp. 316.

13   "The list would grow ..." Introduction, "Nixon's Enemies List," www.paperlessarchives.com

13   Newman: "My single highest honor ..." *Time*, Oct. 7, 2002.

17   Colson and his staff ..., I.R.S. report, p. 1.

18   IRS refused to launch audits ... Wikipedia entry, "Nixon's enemies lists."

18   Tax audits, I.R.S. report, p. 2.

18   "Not politically responsive ..." and "unable to obtain ..." I.R.S. report, p. 2.

18   "... inviting disaster." I.R.S. report p. 4.

18   "papers and tapes donated ..." I.R.S. report, pp. 13.

18   Nixon tax problem ... "Nixon Reported to Pay Back Tax," *The New York Times*, May 1, 1974.

58   G. Gordon Liddy — Wikipedia entry, "Watergate scandal."

58-59   Frank Wills played himself in the 1976 film version of *All the President's Men,* now available on DVD.

59   Arrest of burglars, "Wikipedia entry, "Watergate scandal."

59   John Dean excerpt. *The Nixon Defense,* pp. xvii.

60   ... cub reporter ... *Ernest Hemingway: Cub Reporter.* Matthew J. Bruccoli, ed. x
          Pittsburgh: The University of Pittsburgh Press, 1970.

60   Woodward and Bernstein's work history, *All the President's Men,* pp. 13, 15.

61-64   Timeline of Watergate scandal, Wikipedia entry, "Watergate scandal" and PBS Newshour "The complete Watergate timeline (it took longer than you realize)."

64   The Press, Wikipedia entry, "Watergate scandal."

65   "A source in ..." *All the President's Men,* pp. 71.

65   "phones could be tapped ..." "FBI's No 2 was "Deep Throat": Mark Felt ends 30-Year Mystery of the Post's Watergate source. David Von Drehie, *The Washington Post.* June 1, 2005.

66   "My friend ..." Wikipedia Entry, "Mark Felt."

67   ... charged with crimes, Wikipedia entry, "Watergate scandal."

70   Frost interviews, "Nixon interviews," Wikipedia entry.

About the Author

Thomas Fensch has been publishing books since 1970; he has written 38 previous nonfiction books. They included books about: John Steinbeck, 5; James Thurber, 2; Theodor "Dr. Seuss" Geisel, 2; one each on Ernest Hemingway and Oskar Schindler; the only full biography of John Howard Griffin, the author of *Black Like Me*; one on Trump figures in classic literature; one on George Orwell; and a variety of other nonfiction books.

Fensch taught at the university level for 35 years. He has a doctorate in print communication from Syracuse University and lives outside Richmond, Virginia.

www.ingramcontent.com/pod-product-compliance
Lightning Source LLC
Chambersburg PA
CBHW080625030426
42336CB00018B/3079